The **NO-NONSENSE GUIDE** to

GLOBAL TERRORISM

Jonathan Barker

'Publishers have created lists of short books that discuss the questions that your average [electoral] candidate will only ever touch if armed with a slogan and a soundbite. Together [such books] hint at a resurgence of the grand educational tradition... Closest to the hot headline issues are *The No-Nonsense Guides*. These target those topics that a large army of voters care about, but that politicos evade. Arguments, figures and documents combine to prove that good journalism is far too important to be left to (most) journalists.'

Boyd Tonkin,
The Independent,
London

About the author
Jonathan Barker lives in Toronto where he works as writer and researcher. He taught political science at the University of Toronto for many years. He has also taught at the University of Dar es Salaam and the University of Arizona. He has done research on local politics in Senegal, Tanzania, India and Uganda. His books include *Street-Level Democracy: Political Settings at the Margins of Global Power* (Toronto: Between the Lines and West Hartford, Connecticut: Kumarian, 1999) and *Rural Communities under Stress: Peasant Farmers and the State in Africa*, (Cambridge: Cambridge University Press, 1989). He is currently working on a full-scale textbook with the working title *Understanding Terrorism*.

Other titles in the series
The No-Nonsense Guide to Animal Rights
The No-Nonsense Guide to Climate Change
The No-Nonsense Guide to Conflict and Peace
The No-Nonsense Guide to Fair Trade
The No-Nonsense Guide to Globalization
The No-Nonsense Guide to Human Rights
The No-Nonsense Guide to International Development
The No-Nonsense Guide to International Migration
The No-Nonsense Guide to Islam
The No-Nonsense Guide to Science
The No-Nonsense Guide to Sexual Diversity
The No-Nonsense Guide to Tourism
The No-Nonsense Guide to the United Nations
The No-Nonsense Guide to World Health
The No-Nonsense Guide to World History
The No-Nonsense Guide to World Poverty

About the New Internationalist
The **New Internationalist** is an independent not-for-profit publishing co-operative. Our mission is to report on issues of global justice. We publish informative current affairs and popular reference titles, complemented by world food, photography and gift books as well as calendars, diaries, maps and posters – all with a global justice world view.

If you like this *No-Nonsense Guide* you'll also enjoy the **New Internationalist** magazine. Each month it takes a different subject such as *Trade Justice*, *Permaculture* or *Iran*, exploring and explaining the issues in a concise way; the magazine is full of photos, charts and graphs as well as music, film and book reviews, country profiles, interviews and news.

To find out more about the **New Internationalist**, visit our website at **www.newint.org**

The **NO-NONSENSE GUIDE** to

GLOBAL
TERRORISM

Jonathan Barker

The No-Nonsense Guide to Global Terrorism
Published in the UK in 2008 by New Internationalist™ Publications Ltd
Oxford OX4 1BW, UK
www.newint.org
New Internationalist is a registered trade mark.

First published 2003; second edition 2008.

Cover image: Counter-terrorism excercise, China.
Reuters/China Photos.

© Jonathan Barker 2008

The right of Jonathan Barker to be identified as author of this work has been
asserted in accordance with the Copyright, Designs and Patents Act 1988.

Series editor: Troth Wells
Design by New Internationalist Publications Ltd.

 Printed on recycled paper by T J International, Padstow, Cornwall, UK
who hold environmental accreditation ISO 14001.

British Library Cataloguing-in-Publication Data.
A catalogue record for this book is available from the British Library.

Library of Congress Cataloguing-in-Publication Data.
A catalogue for this book is available from the Library of Congress.

ISBN: 978-1-904456-98-8

Foreword

IN A WORLD that is fraught with crisis and in which transnational and cultural divisions are hardening, Jonathan Barker's wide-ranging yet remarkably succinct *No-Nonsense Guide* is an extraordinarily timely aid to making sense of the complex and often violent responses to the attacks on New York and Washington.

Since those atrocities of 11 September, a 'war on terror' has unfolded across the world. Direct action by US forces or their associates has involved full-scale wars in Afghanistan and Iraq, action in Yemen, Pakistan, Georgia and the Philippines, support for counter-insurgency forces in many countries, and a hardening of legal instruments of control that is almost global in its extent.

There is little evidence that it is working, but this seems to make no difference to the persistent efforts now being made. The al-Qaeda network and its many associates remain active, and grass-roots support for them may even be increasing.

The US is increasing its military spending back towards peak Cold-War levels and has brought in an openly-acknowledged policy of violent pre-emption against movements or states that are seen as enemies. Some states – Iran, Iraq, North Korea, Syria, Libya and Cuba – are even seen as greater or lesser participants in a veritable 'axis of evil', determined to combat a morally certain US as it readily assumes leadership of a movement towards a global civilization rooted in the free market.

Some see the war on terror as an act of desperation, others argue cogently that it relates to an utter determination to regain control of a fractured global system in which the innate vulnerabilities of an advanced state were demonstrated by the attacks in New York and Washington.

Foreword

Whatever the reality, a common theme is a steadfast concern with defeating terrorist groups, coupled with a persistent lack of concern with the underlying motivations of the groups and the contexts within which they draw their considerable support. Nor is much attention given to the much greater and more persistent problem of state terrorism – a mode of extreme political violence that has cost millions rather than thousands of lives in the past half century.

Jonathan Barker's analysis in this book is remarkable in several respects. It places the events of the past few of years in a much wider context, ranging widely over the problems of terrorism of recent decades. It brings together precise descriptions and sharp analysis of the many instances of state terrorism, rightly pointing to the frequent involvement of western states.

Furthermore, it shows how terrorism and its response constrain democratic political discussion and action. Political rights and liberties are restricted and a moralistic language is employed that can even mirror that of the terrorist.

Most significantly, this book puts the atrocities of 11 September, and the subsequent military responses, in the context of a divided world in which the increasing socio-economic divisions are leading to a degree of bitterness and alienation that is rarely recognized in Western states.

This book is an excellent contribution to our understanding of the issues and deserves a very wide readership. In particular, it should be required reading for any Western security analyst, policy adviser or politician concerned in any way with responding to events since 11 September 2001.

Paul Rogers
Professor of Peace Studies
Bradford University, UK

CONTENTS

Introduction

TERRORISM HAS CHANGED since the urgency of the topic forced itself upon me in 2001. Issues of political participation in developing countries were my main passion, but the attacks in New York and Washington obliged me to acknowledge a side of politics I had preferred to ignore. Violence and intimidation, I had figured, were always an ugly presence. But their very universality made it safe to set them aside. Now terrorism and war against it became central themes of political talk and government policy. I was faced with disturbing questions. The events of 11 September 2001 imposed the first ones: What people undertake such shattering crimes? What makes them choose to murder ordinary people leading ordinary lives? I had somehow ignored a grim side of political participation that demanded attention. How dangerous was it? What could be done about it? But the response to terrorism, much of which seemed to me to be disastrously misguided, took the questioning in other directions. What made the US Government so ready to make terrorism a question of national survival that required a military solution? What ideas about terrorists and terrorism guided policy in the US and elsewhere? What narratives took hold of public understanding and shaped political action and debate? Finally, my preoccupation with terrorism brought me back to my earlier interest: What was the effect of terrorism and counter-terrorism on political participation?

But delving into these questions was fraught with difficulty. An immediate problem was cynicism. Could any official statement or mainstream news item be taken at face value? Conspiracy theories could hardly be ignored since terrorism, including state terrorism, always involves deception and hidden agents. But conspiracy talk tended to ignore real complexity and uncertainty and it pulled talented analysts away from other important political issues and called into question the credibility of all political speech. I decided to be careful and skeptical, but to leave the pursuit of conspiracy to others.

Even when gathering basic facts I faced obstacles. I had to recall that governments shape and even manufacture news about terrorism and that terrorist organizations, too, create news coverage that will further their aims. Interpretations were also suspect. I was struck by how quickly commentators in serious newspapers and magazines found in the rubble of terrorist blasts corroboration of their long-held positions. Eventually, I was heartened to find several researchers and observers with new and revealing insights about the changing context of terrorism and the evolving ways international terrorist groups operate.

Another obstacle derives from the very emotions that terrorist acts are often designed to produce: fear and hatred. The expression of hatred in politics reached depths not seen since the time of Nazi menace and Red scares. A good portion of political speech was soon devoted to clarifying exactly who one hates, predictably poisoning the well of mutual recognition that waters political dialogue and diplomatic accommodation. My own response has been to try not to be dismissive of anyone's ideas, but to evaluate them on their merits. Fortunately some penetrating thinking has begun to enter the dialog. I hope this book will push that process ahead.

We need clear understanding of the dangers of terrorism and counter-terrorism to assure security and freedom – and to defend and enlarge the ability of people everywhere to work together democratically to resolve the problems that loom largest in their lives.

Jonathan Barker
Toronto

1 Questions and standpoints

The attacks of 11 September 2001 on the World Trade Center and the Pentagon raised disturbing questions. Subsequent attacks in Bali, Madrid, London and elsewhere, and wars in Afghanistan and Iraq waged in the name of counter-terrorism, only deepened the questioning. Is terrorism a growing threat? Has the response to the attacks lowered or raised hostility across a global divide? Do anti-terrorism measures protect or undermine democratic practices?

BEFORE THE PERFECTION of dynamite by Alfred Nobel in the 1860s it was difficult for a few attackers to kill people indiscriminately and in large numbers. In the 1790s it took the resources of Robespierre's Government in revolutionary France to round up hundreds of thousands of suspects and turn the guillotine, with its official toll of 17,000 executions, into the symbol and the instrument of the officially-proclaimed policy of 'terror' against the enemies of the revolution. The conservative British politician, Edmund Burke, was among the first to use the terms 'terrorism' and 'terrorist'. He wanted to draw attention to the murderous excesses of the Jacobin state and its 'strong corps of irregulars... those hell-hounds called terrorists... let loose on the people'. In the late 1800s Russian anarchists adopted the term for their own non-state use, describing proudly as 'terrorism' their stabbing, strangling or shooting of selected state officials. Since then few have claimed the label; it has been reserved as a term of abuse to describe one's enemies.

Dynamite raised the power of terrorism beyond targeted assassination and it soon became the terrorists' weapon of choice. The mass production of light automatic rifles (M16, AK47 and similar models) after the Second World War added guns to the repertoire of weapons for multiple killing. Both states and non-state groups continue to make ample use of such weapons for terrorist acts.[1]

Terrorism by non-state groups (I will call it 'group terrorism' where needed to avoid confusion) and state terrorism are both important parts of the story. For some purposes finer distinctions are necessary: rightwing, leftwing, anarchist, irredentist nationalist, anti-colonial nationalist, religious, internal state, external state, colonial, state terrorism by proxy, and many more. Recently there has been debate about whether, and when, to use the adjectives Muslim, Islamic, Islamist, jihadist, Salafist, and even Islamo-fascist to refer to the most noted current type of terrorism.

A few brief accounts illustrate varieties of terrorist incidents that have long been familiar to modern politics.

1 Suicide bombing: *Before he left the village that night, 24-year-old Nabil sorted out a few things. At four in the afternoon he went to see his cousin Abdullah Halabiyeh, who lived next door, and paid him back the $15 he had owed him for a year and a half. Then he cleaned his new car... At 6pm, he handed over a petition he had been gathering to get the local council to tar the road outside the family home and told Abdullah to keep hassling them... And then at 9.30pm he went to his bare room to pray.*

'He was crying and saying Qur'an... And I asked him [why he was] making a long time in the praying and he said nothing – and smiled,' Abdullah said.

Abdullah watched him drive off around 10pm. Nabil's final destination was only 10 minutes away so he must have stopped somewhere to pick up his companion and fellow villager Osama Bahar, and the explosives they would wrap round their waists. At about 11.30pm they walked into Jerusalem's crowded Ben Yehuda pedestrian shopping mall and, in the midst of the bright lights and chatting teenagers, pulled the detonators. Nails and shrapnel, mixed in with the explosives, mutilated anyone within 20 feet of these two exploding human bombs. Eleven Israelis were killed and 37 injured. There was little of the bombers left to pick up....[2]

2 Disappearance: *On 27 January 1977 Dagmar Hagelin, then 17 years old, traveled across Buenos Aires, Argentina, to visit her friend, Norma Burgos. But Norma had been arrested the previous day. In her apartment seven military men lay in ambush. Led by Alfredo Astiz, a young naval officer and agent in the military regime's 'dirty war' against its leftist opponents, they were hoping to nab other subversives. When Astiz tried to grab Dagmar, she turned and ran. Alfredo and another soldier gave chase. When Dagmar stretched her lead to about 100 feet (30 meters) Alfredo knelt, took aim with his regulation pistol and with a single shot brought her down. The soldiers commandeered a taxi at gunpoint, put the bleeding girl in the trunk and sped away. She was never seen again.*[3]

3 Targeted state terror: *On 19 May 1994 in San Salvador someone broke into the offices shared by the Salvadoran Women's Movement (MSM) and the Madeleine Lagadec Human Rights Center. The following day unidentified gunmen killed Alexander Rodas Abarca as he was guarding the offices. He was a reserve member of the National Police and member of the security group for the Farabundo Martí National Liberation Front (FMLN), a guerrilla movement that became a political party under the terms of the 1992 Peace Accords. The directors of the two organizations dismissed robbery as the motive for the break-in since nothing of any value was taken. They said, however, that the staff of the office had seen people and vehicles watching the premises for some days before the incident.*[4]

4 Co-ordinated car bomb attacks: *Late on 12 May [2003] two cars, a pickup, and an SUV drove through Riyadh, Saudi Arabia. Around 11.15pm one of the cars, packed with explosives and five or six terrorists, quietly attempted to gain entry to the back gate area of the Dorrat Al Jadawel, a compound owned by the London-based MBI International and Partners' subsidiary Jadawel International.*

As the guards approached to inspect the vehicle, the terrorists opened fire, killing a Saudi Air Force policeman and an unarmed Saudi civilian security guard.... While the terrorists were still attempting to get inside the compound, their massive explosive charge detonated, killing all of the attackers and a Filipino worker. At the Al Hamra Oasis Village and the compound of the Vinnell Corporation (a Virginia-based defense contractor that was training the Saudi National Guard), other assault teams in vehicles loaded with explosives shot their way through the gates and then detonated their bombs, devastating the compounds.

Altogether at least 26 people died, including nine Americans, seven Saudis, three Filipinos, two Jordanians, and one each from Australia, Britain, Ireland, Lebanon and Switzerland. In addition, nine suicide bombers died. More than 160 other people were injured.[5]

These acts are chilling in their familiarity but they illustrate important differences. The suicide bombers aimed to kill and maim dozens among the broad cross-section of people in a popular public mall. The state terrorists openly went after activist youths in one case and in the other hid the state connection in their attack on human rights workers. The car bombers chose protected targets that represented American and European interference in the heartland of Islam for a co-ordinated operation using guns, explosives and suicide terrorists.

Questions and standpoints

Upping the ante

Shootings and bombings have remained regular terrorist methods for many decades in many countries, while other terrorist acts have had periods of frequent use. In the 1980s airplane hijackings, often by persons claiming to have automatic weapons or bombs in their possession, became a recurring technique in the terrorist repertoire. The hijackers would take passengers hostage and bargain with authorities for money, safe passage to a friendly country, the release of comrades, or publicity about their cause. Sometimes airplanes were sabotaged with bombs hidden on board, timed to destroy the craft in the air and kill passengers and crew. Terrorists also used massive car and truck bombs hooked to timers or to remote controls, to kill people and to damage buildings of symbolic importance like the US Marine Barracks in

---

Terrorist incidents in October 2007

Pakistan, 1 October: In the town of Bannu in northwestern Pakistan, a male suicide bomber, disguised as a woman and wearing a burqa, set off a blast that killed at least 15 people and injured 22 others. CNN, *Der Spiegel*

Afghanistan, 2 October: In Kabul, a suicide bomber wearing a *pakul* and a *chador* blew up a police bus, killing 13 officers and civilians on a day that a UN report found that while 76 per cent of all suicide bombings in the country during 2007 had targeted international and Afghan security forces, 143 civilians were killed by those bombs through August. *MSNBC*

Austria, 2 October: Two Bosnians were arrested in an apparent plot to bomb the United States embassy in Vienna. One was arrested after his bag, packed with explosives and several handfuls of nails and screws, set off a metal detector at the entrance to the embassy. *MSNBC*

Iraq, 3 October: The Polish ambassador to Iraq, General Edward Pietrzyk, was injured in an assassination attempt in Baghdad. His convoy was hit by three bombs and was then fired upon. The diplomat had a leg wound and suffered burns in the attack and was evacuated from the scene via a Blackwater helicopter. The attacks killed three in his entourage and two Iraqi civilians and wounded 11 Iraqi civilians. *CNN*

Netherlands, 4 October: In a suicide attack on a police station of the Amsterdam district Slotervaart, Bilal Bajaka, a 22-year-old

Beirut in 1983, the Grand Hotel in Brighton in 1984 during the Conservative Party Conference, or the Murrah Federal Building in Oklahoma City in 1995.

Like suicide bombers, the men who crashed passenger jets into the World Trade Center and the Pentagon on 11 September 2001 were determined to die with their victims, but they added a new wrinkle by employing hijacked airplanes with their loads of volatile fuel as giant exploding missiles. The combination was original, as was the scale of the operation, with intricate planning and special training to deploy four carefully organized teams. The suicide attackers were also unusual for their mature age and their professional credentials. The targets stood as symbols of the global economic and military power of the United States. Al-Qaeda, the transnational network led by Osama bin Laden and Ayman al-Zawahiri, took

---

Amsterdammer of Moroccan origin severely injured two Dutch police officers by stabbing them eight times before he was shot dead by an injured policewoman. Bajaka was in contact with the Hofstad terrorist group and had been visited by Mohammed Bouyeri, the murderer of Theo van Gogh (film director). *Expatica News, Elsevier Nieuws, DutchNews*

India, 14 October: A bomb exploded in the Shingar Cinema in Ludhiana killing at least six people and wounding 20, police said. *Reuters*

Pakistan, 18 October: Twin suicide bombings occured in Karachi near a truck carrying former Prime Minister Benazir Bhutto through a crowded street of supporters, eight hours after her return from exile, despite 20,000 security officers assigned to protect her. There were at least 136 killed and 387 wounded. Bhutto escaped unharmed. (She was killed in a similar attack on 27 December 2007). The Taliban or Al Qaeda were suspected. *MSNBC, CNN*

Israel, 24 October: An off-duty Israeli Defense Force soldier was badly injured and a civilian was slightly injured in a shooting attack on the Trans-Samaria road near the entrance to Ariel. Responsibility for the shooting was claimed by the Al-Aqsa Martyrs' Brigades. *The Bulletin*

United States, 26 October: A pair of improvised explosive devices were thrown at the Mexican Consulate in New York City. The fake grenades were filled with black powder and detonated by fuses causing very minor damage. Police were investigating the connection between this and a similar attack against the British Consulate in New York in 2005. *AP*

years to prepare the operation. It aimed to challenge and weaken the global power of the United States and to drive US influence from the holy places of Islam.[6]

Global ambition was apparent in other attacks, notably the bombing in a tourist district in Bali, Indonesia on 12 March 2002 (202 dead, 164 injured), the bombing of four commuter trains in Madrid on 11 March 2004 (171 dead, 2050 injured) and the bombing in London on 7 July 2005 of three underground trains and one bus (52 dead, 500 injured).

What has changed? Terrorists still favor bombs and assault weapons, but very destructive attacks have become more common and the number of people killed has risen since 2001 even when incidents in Iraq are left out.[7] Multiple co-ordinated teams, powerful remotely controlled bombs to attack vehicles and buildings (especially in Iraq and Afghanistan), and suicide missions have also become common practice in these conflicts. The more frequent use of these modes of terrorism poses a challenge to counter-terrorism strategies. But the big fear, often expressed by US Government officials, is that terrorists will find a way to deploy nuclear, biological or chemical weapons. States, of course, have used these weapons against civilians on several occasions.[8] The 1995 sarin gas attack on the Tokyo subway by the Aum Shinrikyo sect is the main example of a chemical attack by a non-state group, but the method of dispersing the poison was defective and it killed 12 people instead of the thousands intended.[9] The five anthrax letters mailed by persons unknown to media offices in Florida and New York and to two senators in Washington DC in October 2001 also, intentionally or not, failed to disperse the infectious spores to more than a few people (five were killed and 17 more infected).[10]

More important than the actual change of terrorist techniques has been the use of terrorism by groups aiming to change global power relations. It is part of a larger transformation of world patterns of power, communication and culture that is often referred to as globalization, a transformation that has had major consequences for the reactions to terrorism as well as for terrorism itself.

Reactions

The changes in the way terrorism is perceived and the way counter-terrorism is organized have been even more striking than the new developments on the terrorist side of the equation. The mesmerizing images of big Boeings flying through the outer walls of New York's World Trade Center towers and the colossal structures collapsing downward into themselves captured a global audience. They made terrorism a central topic of political news and conversation in the US and around the world. Pictures of shattered entertainment buildings in Bali, wrecked railway cars in Madrid, and smoldering underground trains in London were similarly affecting. These attacks and dozens of others kept the story and the concern alive. But emotions and questions awakened were far from uniform and over time they have evolved.

An enemy that at first seemed to be a set of identifiable haters of America and industrial modernity gradually came to resemble a web of strands of uncertain strength, extending from caves in the remote mountains on the Pakistan/Afghanistan border to middle-class neighborhoods of Europe and America, from mosques in Algeria and Morocco to schools in Indonesia and training camps in the Philippines, from hideouts in Chechnya and Pakistan to safe houses in Iraq. In much of the reporting and official comment the distinction between local conflicts and global threats became fuzzy and whether there was any central control became uncertain. In the western-dominated media an image took hold of a sprawling danger driven by anti-Western animus connected with

Islam. The nature of the danger, what motivates it, and what to do about it became familiar topics of dispute among commentators, political leaders and experts of various kinds.

On the political side, the American position has focused the debate. President Bush has held to the view he put forward in his address to the US Congress on 20 September 2001: 'Why do they hate us? They hate our freedoms – our freedom of religion, our freedom of speech, our freedom to vote and assemble and disagree with each other.'[11] Rudy Giuliani, who was Mayor of New York City in 2001, as candidate in 2007 for the Republican nomination for President took the point one step further. Why do they hate American-style freedom? '[N]ot because of anything bad we have done.... The freedoms we have are in conflict with the perverted, maniacal interpretation of their religion.'[12]

A quite different explanation takes up 'the things we have done' that Giuliani rules out. According to Michael Scheuer, formerly head analyst at the CIA's Bin Laden unit: 'It's American foreign policy that enrages Osama and al-Qaeda, not American culture and society.'[13] They take offense at specific western interventions in predominantly Muslim countries and seek to force changes in those policies. Especially offensive have been the US and Western support for Israel on Palestinian issues, stationing troops in the religious heartland of Islam, and support for governments in Egypt, Saudi Arabia, Algeria and elsewhere seen as hostile to true Islam.

A third viewpoint makes a much more general political argument and sees terrorist attacks as one response among many to the interventionism that has been pursued by powerful countries since the industrial revolution. Just as powerful governments find excuses to invade and subjugate weaker peoples using the violence of armies, movements without military capacity that are determined to fight back against interference by military superpowers are likely to turn to terrorism, just as they always have. The motivation is not new, but the globalization of communication and development of new types of weapons have altered the danger. They have brought new international targets into play and opened the possibility of much more destructive attacks.[14] It should be noted that these views can be evaluated in more than one way. Some Islamists agree that Western culture and Islam are incompatible and express contempt for the materialism and selfishness promoted in Western culture. But for them loyalty to their idea of Islamic law is the highest form of freedom.[15] Likewise some commentators agree that US interventions to protect Western oil supplies and to backstop moderate governments in the Muslim world have stimulated a terrorist response, but they go on to argue that these are legitimate policies that must be defended.[16] Moreover, there are some wide-angle thinkers who agree with the general proposition that the global projection of Western power has bred terrorism, but who reject postcolonial guilt and recommend a confident imperialist presence that is willing to police strategic, but disorderly, regions of the world.[17]

There has been a lively inquiry into why governments and publics respond to terrorist attacks the way they do in the US and elsewhere. The questions about the sources of terrorism and the responses to it are closely linked because terrorist actions and counter-terrorist measures feed off one another. We need to grasp how they interact. For example, several writers have tried to understand how the US Government chose a military-centered counter-terrorism policy that, according to many observers, has not only failed to weaken terrorism but has instead caused the terrorist danger to grow.[18] Both this specific case and the general topic invite deeper investigation because the claims made about them range so widely and often contradict one another. Three interpretations of the US response can be stated briefly: Counter-terrorism was just a cover for enforcing control over key oil supplies.[19] Counter-terrorism was constructed by old Cold Warriors hankering to find a new armed global ideological enemy like Nazism or communism whether it existed or not.[20] Counter-terrorism was designed by a military establishment whose *modus operandi*, inappropriate to the task at hand, is to apply high tech firepower to kill the most enemy soldiers at the lowest cost in casualties.[21] Of course, two or more of these views could be true at the same time.

Several thinkers have tried to fathom the public response. The French social thinker Jean Baudrillard made one of the broadest claims about the spectacular attacks in the US: 'This terrorist imagination – unconsciously – inhabits us all. We have dreamed of this event ... everybody without exception has dreamed of it, because nobody can fail to dream of the destruction of any power that has become hegemonic to that degree...' According to Baudrillard the West's 'moral conscience' gives such enormous symbolic importance to the event because it feels a psychological complicity it cannot acknowledge.[22]

Susan Faludi, looking more narrowly at the American response, finds it resonates with an older narrative of strong men of the frontier protecting their women and children from wanton attacks of natives. The old narrative itself was constructed in response to the actual failures of men to provide such protection. She believes the new counter-terrorist narrative taps into the same motivating imagery and fuels a new assertion of masculine power over women.[23]

Other writers have seen an enveloping shadow of fear spread through the population, making security a major public issue and narrowing participation in public life. Some of them have added that governments have magnified evidence of danger in order to keep the current of public fear flowing and ease acceptance of new claims to widening government control over travel, information and interrogation.[24]

Now that terrorism has led the political agenda of many governments for six or seven years, we can begin to sort through the varying claims about terrorism and counter-terrorism to form a realistic picture of how they work and how they relate to one another, but there are a few distinctive difficulties of the topic to address.

Feeling and thinking

The very first thing to confront in writing or reading about terrorism is so obvious that it often escapes mention, yet it stands as one of the obstacles to clear thinking, adequate discussion and good analysis. One has to think about ugly events, horrifying actions that kill and injure unsuspecting people going about their daily lives. One has to focus on the terrible effects of deaths, injuries and destruction on those whose worlds and bodies are torn to pieces by explosions designed to kill, maim and frighten. One has to reflect on the people who undertake such unthinkable actions, on those who design and plan atrocities, actually hoping for deadly results. Like the victims, like the survivors and like us, these terrorists are human beings. The questions are unavoidable: What makes us humans capable of such acts? Are there conditions under which I might do something similar? Reflecting on terrorist acts is the stuff of blame and tears, raised voices and raised fists, sleeplessness and nightmares.

Because the topic is so taxing most people have grown weary of trying to deepen their comprehension and to stay abreast of changes in the threat. Yet in the years since 2001 the flow of information on the topic has continued to be strong. The best of it reveals that changes in terrorism make it dangerous to stick with old conceptions.

That terrorist acts arouse strong emotions is no accident. A core purpose of 'propaganda by the deed,' dating from the 19th century anarchists, has been to sway the minds and emotions of people. Many recent terrorist operations reveal skillful attention to the use of media reports and images to engage in different ways the emotions of the people the terrorists see as their friends and those they see as enemies. Precisely because it engages our deepest feelings and challenges our moral commitments, terrorism takes on a political potency rivaled only by war and by deep-seated differences of ideology, religion or identity – commitments with which it is often connected. Terrorism is often associated with war or fear of war and with ideological positioning, so political agendas bristle forth in most communication on the subject.

Recognizing the emotional force of the topic, government-friendly experts often try to gather support for official policy and burnish feelings of righteousness rather than strive to enlighten understanding and challenge prejudice. They often place the actions, ideas, people and organizations denoted by the terms 'terrorism' and 'terrorist' beyond the boundaries of reason, ethics and interest that govern ordinary politics. A writer for a publication of the Hoover Institution, a conservative think-tank, praises the President for identifying the targets of the US as 'the evil ones': he explains, 'our enemy has already dehumanized himself... You do not try to appease them, or persuade them, or reason with them. You try, on the contrary, to outwit them, to vanquish them, to kill them. You behave with them in the same manner that you would deal with a fatal epidemic – you try to wipe it out.'[25]

The words 'terrorism' and 'terrorist' are themselves pejoratives. Nowhere is the political loading more evident than in the refusal of governments to recognize their own terrorist actions. Those who speak for governmental authority speak with conviction about fighting the evil of terrorism. They enumerate the death and damage perpetrated by terrorist bombs while holding silence about the death and damage to civilians and bystanders caused by the bombs they use to fight terrorism. Moreover, government agencies and their proxies all too often kill and frighten their own citizens, as happened when France's revolutionary government began devouring its own makers. Such killing can be a core policy of relatively stable governments, as Hannah Arendt pointed out in her analysis of Nazi Germany and Stalinist USSR in her book *Origins of Totalitarianism*.[26] In recent years many governments are known to have supported death squads to eliminate and frighten opponents, and some employ similar techniques against the people of other countries in order to weaken regimes they do not like or to assist regimes they favor that face internal opposition.

The United States has been unusually open in admitting its use of secret operations. A law Congress passed in 1991, requiring the State Department to release documents about covert operations in the volumes it publishes about diplomatic activity 30 years after the event, has brought many interventions to light. For example, a document written by US Ambassador Marshall Green during the killings of hundreds of thousands of alleged communists in Indonesia, in the wake of the US-approved coup that brought General Suharto to power in 1965, reveals that a list of communist leaders prepared by the US Embassy was given to the Indonesian Government in December 1965. Green writes, it 'is apparently being used by Indonesian security authorities who seem to lack even the simplest overt information on PKI [Indonesian Communist Party] leadership.' Another document shows that on 2 December 1965, Green endorsed a covert payment of 50 million rupiah ($5,400) to the Kap-Gestapu movement leading the repression.[27] US officials usually defend such operations as legitimate responses to requests for help from friendly governments or legitimate self-defense against foreign threats. They certainly do not call them terrorism.

Non-state terrorists are no strangers to posing and hypocrisy. They typically have a smaller amplifier than do established governments, although some now make effective use of the internet. They, too, usually declare that their violence is not terror, but warfare. Some groups invent new names for themselves and lay claim to actions they did not commit in order to inflate their numbers and importance.[28]

It is difficult to communicate in a straightforward way on a topic so morally polarized and so politically manipulated. Most people are highly suspicious of at least one side in the conflict. Moreover, the facts are ugly and the proclaimed dangers are hair-raising. Yet the rewards of grappling with issues of terrorism are real and valuable. We gain a better understanding of the dangers we face from a frightening kind of violence and a deeper appreciation of the challenges facing politics, especially democratic politics. Many may find that the direct dangers of terrorism are smaller than they had imagined, but that the challenges to democracy are greater than they had thought. In these tough times we need to feel, we need to talk and we need to think. We can do all three at the same time. Such is the premise of this work.

A definition that works

Writers on terrorism frequently imply that laboring to define the term is pointless. They complain that hundreds of definitions have been proposed. They like to cite the dictum 'one person's terrorist is another person's freedom fighter,' suggesting that to call someone a terrorist is to say no more than that one opposes their motivating cause. Much popular understanding, encouraged by common political use, takes the same position. People understand that the planners of the political violence carried out by non-governmental groups or by government agencies or their proxies always claim their cause is just. Governments that employ the dark arts of murder and sabotage, often via proxy organizations, will never acknowledge that they are using terrorism. Those who speak for organizations that regularly use terror tactics

Why terrorism is hard to define

There appears to be agreement across most of the nations [with legal systems based upon the common law]... that the concept refers to political, religious or ideologically-motivated violence that causes harm to people or property, intended either to coerce a civilian population or government, or to instill fear in the population or a certain part of it. However, if a definition is expressed at this level of abstraction... it would extend to (and... potentially criminalize)... civil disobedience, public protest and industrial action... These types of activities should be excluded from any definition of terrorism.

Ben Golder and George Williams, 'What is "Terrorism"? Problems of Legal Definition', in *UNSW Law Journal*, Vol 27 (2) pp 288-289.

Peoples' struggle including armed struggle against foreign occupation, aggression, colonialism, and hegemony, aimed at liberation and self-determination in accordance with the principles of international law shall not be considered a terrorist crime.

The Organization of Islamic Conference Convention on Combating International Terrorism [1998] Annex to Resolution No 59/26-P.

By any generally applicable standard... state terrorism is vastly more destructive than anti-state and individual and small group terrorism. This is the basis for distinguishing between the two as 'wholesale' versus 'retail' terrorism.

Edward S Herman, 'What is Terrorism? On the Pre-eminence of State Terrorism,' *Z Magazine Online*, February 2006.

avoid the term and claim they are resisting oppression and fighting for justice. Reuters' press service, although it refers to terrorism and counter-terrorism in general, does not 'use the word terrorist without attribution to qualify specific individuals, groups or events.' Its grounds? 'This is part of a wider and long-standing policy of avoiding the use of emotive terms.' Without a clear and pertinent definition the words 'terrorist' and 'terrorism' are counters in propaganda wars that

Three definitions of terrorism

[T]he US State Department... defines terrorism as 'premeditated, politically motivated violence perpetrated against non-combatant targets by subnational groups or clandestine agents, usually intended to influence an audience.'

Foreign Policy Association Newsletter, citing Title 22 of the *United States Code*, Section 2656f(d).

'... criminal acts intended or calculated to provoke a state of terror in the general public, a group of persons or particular persons for political purposes are in any circumstance unjustifiable, whatever the considerations of a political, philosophical, ideological, racial, ethnic, religious or other nature that may be invoked to justify them.'

UN, GA Res. 51/210 'Measures to eliminate international terrorism', 1999.

'Terrorism is an anxiety-inspiring method of repeated violent action, employed by (semi-) clandestine individual, group or state actors, for idiosyncratic, criminal or political reasons, whereby – in contrast to assassination – the direct targets of violence are not the main targets. The immediate human victims of violence are generally chosen randomly (targets of opportunity) or selectively (representative or symbolic targets) from a target population, and serve as message generators. Threat- and violence-based communication processes between terrorist (organization), (imperiled) victims, and main targets are used to manipulate the main target (audience(s)), turning it into a target of terror, a target of demands, or a target of attention, depending on whether intimidation, coercion, or propaganda is primarily sought.'

Schmid 1988.

obscure analysis of the frightful acts they are often used to describe.[29]

Fortunately there is a simple and straightforward definition that corresponds to the idea of terrorism that most people hold. It has three elements: violence threatened or employed; against civilian targets; for political objectives. Boaz Ganor proposes that 'terrorism is the intentional use of, or threat to use violence against civilians or against civilian targets, in order to attain political aims.' Unlike many other definitions this one applies to governments (and their agencies and proxies) as well as to non-governmental groups and individuals. It excludes nonviolent political actions such as protests, strikes, demonstrations, tax revolts and civil disobedience. It also excludes violent actions against military and police forces. Thus most acts of guerrilla fighters and urban rioters are not terrorism.[30]

According to our definition only actions are unambiguously terrorist or non-terrorist. People and organizations and strategies make more or less use of terrorism often in conjunction with other kinds of political action. How groups and states mix terrorism with other kinds of action is important information for counter-terrorism policy. Can the organization be induced to abandon terrorism in favor of politics? If so, labeling the whole organization as terrorist may be a mistake. Still, organizations that are designed to carry out terrorist operations can properly be called terrorist organizations and the people who plan and implement the actions are terrorists.

The definition opens the door to fundamental questions about the circumstances under which people, groups and states adopt (and also abandon) terrorist methods; the kind of people, groups and states that are attracted to terrorist methods; and the consequences of terrorist actions for victims and for perpetrators. But it does not load the painful weight of

Array of terrorisms

There are many kinds of targets, weapons, groups, and supporting infrastructures. Every terrorist attack brings together a specific combination of these elements.

ATTACKS
- kidnapping
- hostage-taking
- suicide bombing
- drive-by shooting
- targeted assassination
- air piracy

TARGETS
- journalists
- oil tankers
- abortion clinics
- tourists
- food supplies
- embassies
- public gatherings
- immigrants
- human rights workers

WEAPONS
- AK 47
- car bomb
- sarin gas
- dirty bomb
- shoulder-fired missile
- anthrax
- airplane as missile

GOALS
- revenge
- free prisoners
- political independence
- boost followers' morale
- publicize demands
- weaken government

GROUPS
- secret state agency
- religious militants
- neo-nazis
- proxy for state
- nationalists
- official state agency
- left-wing militants

INFRASTRUCTURE
- money laundering
- counter intelligence
- safe houses
- training camps
- weapons suppliers
- funding sources

Jonathan Barker

28

all violence on terrorism. By focusing on a special kind of violence – violence against civilians for political ends – the definition acknowledges that many other kinds of violence surround politics.

In principle this definition can also distinguish terrorist violence (that targets civilians) from the violence of warfare that is sanctioned by the laws of war (that require measures to protect civilians and prisoners of war). Unfortunately, the records of guerrilla wars and other modern wars show that both government-organized armies and guerrilla fighters often target civilians. Terrorism, much of it state terrorism, has been integral to warfare between governments and guerrillas, just as it has been part and parcel of state-on-state warfare. Removing terrorism from warfare is as big a challenge as is removing it from politics. It is a large topic in its own right that this book will only touch upon.

With this definition as a starting point we can begin a discussion of terrorism, but its terms will require further elaboration. What counts as violence and as threat of violence? Who counts as civilian? What counts as a political objective? Lawmakers work these terms to design laws against terrorism that suit their purposes, often casting a very wide net indeed. Analysts and activists have some scope to shape the discussion to fit their biases and to take account of changes in patterns of violence. Discussing these terms is meaningful and relevant to understanding how to protect effective broad-based participation in democratic politics. When do religious or cultural claims become 'political'? When does state power or citizen action cross the line and become violence? Which officials count as 'combatants' as opposed to civilians? When does violent conflict cross the line from terrorism and counter-terrorism to qualify as warfare?

The definition allows one to raise the question

of whether under some circumstances terrorism is justified on the same lines that some wars are reasoned just and some torture legitimate (see page 97). If the objective is morally valid, the balance of suffering favorable and the likelihood of success great would not violence against civilians be morally justified?

More also needs to be said about the use of fear as a whip to bring about change in policies and organizations. What are the effects of the fear of terrorism? For what purposes is the manipulation of fear a useful tactic? The definition gets a vital discussion started.

Questions

Since 11 September 2001 a host of experts has emerged who seemed to have thought about the hard questions terrorism raises. Additionally, hard-working journalists and researchers have dug into crucial aspects of the current situation. This guide seeks to take advantage of the best work of all these communicators, but its standpoint differs from most of them in important ways. They tend to ignore state terrorism and to focus narrowly on the danger that they believe group terrorism – especially Islamist terrorism – poses to the US and to the West. Most commentators make attacks by Islamist terrorists, implacably opposed to Western values, the core danger. Less frequently encountered is the view that government responses that betray Western and American political traditions of civil and political liberties are the primary danger. This book takes the position that both are important concerns but that state terrorism, nationalist terrorism, and terrorism of left and right also need consideration. Moreover, terrorism and counter-terrorism do not stand isolated from major global trends such as environmental change, international population movements, transnational political networks and the operational weaknesses of many governments. We aim to raise questions about all these matters, both about where terrorism comes from and where it takes us.

How have political ideologies and religious beliefs fed into terrorism? Does the extreme and growing inequality between and within countries cause terrorism? Does the failure of some peoples and cultures to better their material living conditions make them vulnerable to terrorism? Equally important are questions about outcomes and consequences. How do terrorism and counter-terrorism affect politics, popular politics in particular? Could the very actions, including the 'war on terrorism,' that are intended to defend democracy in the US and other industrial countries undermine democracy in poorer and weaker countries? Could they also be working against democratic activism in the industrial North?

The connection of terrorism with violence, personal and society-wide security, and painful injustice makes it particularly demanding to think about. These qualities generate emotional reactions. Paradoxically, the emotional coloring of the terrorism discussions offers a real opportunity to advance understanding once we get past the initial barriers to discussion and analysis. How can we really understand something we do not care about? Too many topics of real importance in our world today are met with so little passion that changes in understanding, and therefore changes in conscious action, are unlikely. Terrorism is different. If we can overcome a reluctance to look directly at some bruising realities, examining terrorism may carry us deeper than we realize into questions about the adequacy of our political institutions and leaders to the problems the world faces.

1 Gideon Burrows, *Kalashnikov AK47*, Trigger Issues, New Internationalist/ Between the Lines, 2007. 2 Kevin Toolis, 'Where suicide is a cult', *The Observer*, 16 December 2001. 3 Adapted from Marcus Gee, 'The Dirty War's Dirtiest Soldier', *The Globe and Mail*, 10 June 2002, which cites 'Nunca Mas', the official report on the crimes of Argentina's Dirty War. 4 Amnesty International online, www.amnesty.org/ailib/intcam/

Questions and standpoints

cemexico/salvador.htm **5** Adapted from http://en.wikipedia.org/wiki/ Riyadh_Compound_Bombings consulted 19 September 2007. **6** Lawrence Wright, *The Looming Tower: Al-Qaeda and the Road to 9/11*, Knopf, 2006. **7** Carl Conetta, *War & Consequences: Global Terrorism Has Increased Since 9/11 Attacks*, updated 25 September 2006, Project on Defense Alternatives Briefing Memo #38, Commonwealth Institute, 2006, www. comw.org/pda/0609bm38.html. **8** Chronology of State Use and Biological and Chemical Weapons Control, James Martin Center for Nonproliferation Studies website http://cns.miis.edu/research/cbw/pastuse.htm **9** Kyle B Olson, 'Aum Shinrikyo: Once and Future Threat?' *Emerging Infectious Diseases 5*, no 4 (July-August 1999): 513–16. **10** The fantasy link: 9/11, anthrax, and the Iraq war, OpenDemocracy, 19 September 2006, opendemocracy.net **11** White House website www.whitehouse.gov/ news/releases/2001/09/print/20010920-8.html **12** Roger Simon, Giuliani warns of 'new 9/11' if Dems win, Politico, Apr 24, 2007 Updated: 26 April 2007, www.politico.com/news/stories/0407/3684.html **13** Michael Scheuer, *Imperial Hubris: Why the West is Losing the War on Terror*, Potomac Books, 2004. **14** Audrey Kurth Cronin, 'Behind the Curve: Globalization and International Terrorism', *International Security* 27, no 3, Winter 2002/2003: 30–58. **15** Audrey Kurth Cronin, 'Behind the Curve: Globalization and International Terrorism', *International Security* 27, no 3, Winter 2002/2003: 30–58. **16** Michael Klare, 'Beyond the Age of Petroleum', *The Nation*, 12 November 2007. **17** Robert Kagan, 'End of Dreams, Return of History: International Rivalry and American Leadership', *Policy Review*, no. 144 (August/September 2007). **18** Paul Rogers, *Why We're Losing the War on Terror*, Polity, 2007. **19** Michael Meacher, 'This war on terrorism is bogus', *The Guardian*, 6 September 2003. **20** Stephen Holmes, *The Matador's Cape: America's Reckless Response to Terror*, Cambridge University Press, 2007. **21** Christopher Bolkcom and Kenneth Katzman, *Military Aviation: Issues and Options for Combating Terrorism and Counterinsurgency*, CRS Report for Congress, Congressional Research Service, Library of Congress, 2005, www.fas. org/man/crs/RL32737.pdf **22** Jean Baudrillard, 'L'esprit du terrorisme', *Le Monde*, 3 November 2001. **23** Susan Faludi, *The Terror Dream: Fear and Fantasy in Post-9/11 America*, Metropolitan Books, 2007. **24** David L Altheide, *Terrorism and the Politics of Fear*, AltaMira Press, 2006. **25** Lee Harris, 'Al Qaeda's Fantasy Ideology', *Policy Review*, no 114 (August and September 2002). **26** Hannah Arendt, *The Origins of Totalitarianism*, 2nd ed, World Publishing Company, Meridian, 1958. **27** National Security Archive, Foreign Relations of the United States, 1964-68 Vol XXVI, www.fas.org/sgp/advisory/state/NSAEBB52/NSAEBB52.html **28** Gabriel Weimann, www.terror.net: How Modern Terrorism Uses the Internet, Special Report No 116, United States Institute of Peace, Washington DC, March 2004. **29** http://blogs.reuters.com/blog/2007/06/13/when-does-reuters-use-the-word-terrorist-or-terrorism **30** Boaz Ganor, 'Defining Terrorism: Is One Man's Terrorist Another Man's Freedom Fighter?' The International Policy Institute for Counter-terrorism, 23 September 1998, www.ict.org.il

2 Dangers and fears

Terrorism has become a preoccupation of government leaders around the world. You find it in speeches, laws, budgets and military doctrine. Intelligence and security agencies collaborate more closely, with the US supplying training and hardware where they are lacking. The danger is real, but officials often exaggerate it. One threat requires realistic attention: groups that seek to deploy biological, chemical or nuclear weapons in attacks which would be truly catastrophic.

SINCE THE EVENTS of 11 September 2001, US political leaders have been warning of the continuing high danger of terrorist outrages. In March 2002 a US counter-terrorism official told *Time* magazine: 'It's going to be worse, and a lot of people are going to die. I don't think there's a damn thing we're going to be able to do about it.'

Officials anticipated a frighteningly wide range of attacks: food contamination, water supply poisoning, Hiroshima-size urban nuclear explosions, ocean tankers loaded with liquefied natural gas detonated in port cities, and bombings or suicide missions against buildings, bridges, airplanes, power plants, theme parks, monuments – wherever people gather. Terrorism experts noted the vulnerability of many targets, the cheapness and wide availability of explosives, and the possible use of peaceful contrivances like passenger planes and nuclear generating plants as weapons. 'We're as vulnerable today as we were on 9/10 or 9/12,' said presidential counselor Karen Hughes, 'we just know more.'[1] The US suffered no large-scale terrorist attack for the next six years, but officials frequently remind the public that the danger persists, now from 'home grown' terrorists and decentralized cells that are difficult to identify and monitor. Officials in many other countries, especially those that have experienced attacks, speak the same way.

Cheap and destructive

Like other violent crimes, terrorist attacks require a weapon, an opportunity and a motive. Most attacks in recent years still use weapons that are inexpensive and easy to find: guns and bombs. The outlay for destroying a large building, damaging a mass transit hub, or blowing up a crowded market is but a very

---

Warnings

30 May 2004 – Attorney General John Ashcroft warned of 'credible intelligence from multiple sources' pointing to an al-Qaeda attack in coming months. But he and FBI Director Robert Mueller conceded that they know almost nothing about what form an attack might take.
US News and World Report

30 August 2005 – Another big terrorist attack is imminent in Indonesia, its President, Susilo Bambang Yudhoyono, has warned. The bombing was likely to happen in Jakarta over the next two months, Dr Yudhoyono told a conference of newspaper editors yesterday... 'We know the terrorist cells are still active, they are still hiding, recruiting, networking, trying to find new funding and even planning... for another strike.'
Sydney Morning Herald

6 November 2005 – Australian authorities have received specific intelligence that terrorists are planning an attack on the country, Prime Minister John Howard said Wednesday, calling on lawmakers to increase the powers of Australia's intelligence agencies. Howard refused to give any details of the threat, saying he did not want to jeopardize counter-terror operations...
Associated Press

2 January 2007 – In what has become an annual tradition of prognostications, religious broadcaster Pat Robertson predicted Tuesday that a terrorist attack on the United States would result in 'mass killing' late in 2007... 'The Lord didn't say nuclear. But I do believe it will be something like that.'
Associated Press

21 April 2007 – The US and Australia have warned of an imminent terrorist attack in the Philippines, where seven hostages were this

---

small fraction of the expense of building or rebuilding it, not to mention the emotional and material cost of lost lives and damaged families, communities, businesses and whole economies. The operation that bore brutal fruit on 11 September 2001 cost maybe $500,000.[2] The compensation paid out from insurance, government, and charity for people killed and injured and for businesses damaged in New York City totaled $38 billion and that does not include damage to the Pentagon.[3] In 2001 alone the attacks cost the Gross

---

week beheaded by militants. In an advisory to its citizens the US embassy said an attack could take place anywhere on Mindanao, in the south of the Philippines ... 'over the next several days'.
BBC News

11 May 2007 – American and German officials fear a terrorist attack against U.S. military personnel or American tourists is imminent in Germany... 'The information behind the threat is very real,' ABC quoted a senior U.S. official as saying. 'The danger level is high. We are part of the global threat by Islamist terrorism,' German Interior Minister Wolfgang Schäuble told reporters.
ABC News

5 November 2007 – Extremists are grooming children and teenagers to plot terrorist attacks against Britain, the head of the counter-intelligence agency MI5 said Monday... 'Terrorists are methodically and intentionally targeting young people and children in this country... They are radicalizing, indoctrinating and grooming young, vulnerable people to carry out acts of terrorism.'
Associated Press

26 January 2008 – The threat of additional terror attacks within the US, as well as on American citizens and interests abroad, is very real. Both the Government, and the terrorists themselves, warn of more attacks. Each repeatedly advise you to increase your threat awareness and stay informed. AlertsUSA helps you manage your risk, regardless of your location, with timely notification of substantial terrorist threats, warnings, advisories and other events and incidents of national significance – sent direct to your mobile device.
www.alertsusa.com/index.htm

Domestic Product (GDP) as much as $75 billion. Over the next two years the defense budget shot up $100 billion. If the cost of the action was $500,000 and the short-term damage is valued at $200 billion then the 'rate of destructive return' was 400,000 to one.

Over the longer term there is a huge increase in the portion of the economy devoted to protecting wealth rather than producing it. A Canadian Government economist writing in his personal capacity estimated the global hit from the rise in terrorism to be a 0.25 per cent reduction in global economic growth.[4] But attention must also be given to the impact of the shift in economic activity, including research and development, to war and security and away from poverty, environment, health and other pressing issues.

The war on terrorism in all its facets has raised the cost to terrorists of getting weapons and traveling, but the number of potential targets is very large and only a few of them can be carefully guarded. It is hard to see how the low cost of weapons and the availability of opportunity can be altered fundamentally. What then about motive?

Al-Qaeda is now less a command center than one organized component of Islamist activism that is willing to support and undertake terrorist attacks against those they regard as enemies of the faith. Osama Bin Laden and Ayman al-Zawahiri remain influential voices for recruiting supporters and activists and formulating an overall direction. Their video- and audio-recordings seek to create and to strengthen motives for more terrorist attacks. They express disgust at the continued presence of Western forces in the holy lands of Islam, opposition to the US-led military action in Iraq and Afghanistan, and anger at the plight of the Palestinian people. Opinion polling in Muslim countries suggests that al-Qaeda is cultivating fertile ground; a large current of opinion is critical of the US. Gallup interviewed almost 10,000 people during

Muslim view
Most Muslims are against terrorism.

Suicide bombing and other violence against civilians (Muslim respondents only).

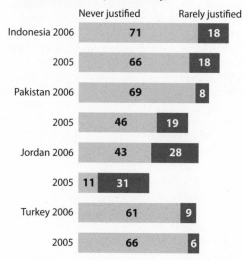

	Never justified	Rarely justified
Indonesia 2006	71	18
2005	66	18
Pakistan 2006	69	8
2005	46	19
Jordan 2006	43	28
2005	11	31
Turkey 2006	61	9
2005	66	6
Germany 2006	83	6
France 2006	64	19
Great Britain 2006	70	9
Spain 2006	69	9
Egypt 2006	45	25
Nigeria 2006	28	23

World Public Opinion.org www.worldpublicopinion.org/pipa/articles/international_security_bt/221.php?nid=&id=&pnt=221&lb=brme

Dangers and fears

December 2001 and January 2002 in its first ever large-scale opinion polling in Indonesia, Iran, Jordan, Kuwait, Lebanon, Morocco, Pakistan, Saudi Arabia and Turkey. The dominant image of the US was a country that is 'ruthless, aggressive, conceited, arrogant, easily provoked and biased.'[5] A Pew research poll in 2006 confirmed that a negative view had persisted. 'In the five majority Muslim countries (Egypt, Indonesia, Jordan, Pakistan, and Turkey), as well as Nigeria, at least 40 per cent of Muslims characterize Westerners as arrogant, violent, greedy, and immoral; meanwhile, relatively few say Westerners are generous or honest. Muslims in these countries are also especially likely to say Westerners are selfish...'[6] Moreover, surveys in late 2006 and early 2007 in Egypt, Morocco, Pakistan, and Indonesia found that '[v]ery large majorities believe the United States seeks to undermine Islam and large majorities even believe it wants to spread Christianity in the region. About the same numbers think a key US goal is to maintain access to oil. While majorities perceive the United States as seeking to prevent terrorist attacks, this is not seen as the primary purpose of the war on terror.'[7]

Historically, local and regional grievances are more common sources of terrorism than the global ones that now grab attention. Certain anti-colonial nationalist movements after World War Two used violence against civilians: for example, the National Liberation Front (FLN) in Algeria and Mau Mau (the Land and Freedom Army) in Kenya. Tamils in Sri Lanka, Palestinians in the Middle East, Basques in Spain, Corsicans in France, Catholics in Northern Ireland, Kurds in Iraq and Turkey, and Sikhs in India are groups that have been associated with episodes of terrorism in nationalist movements seeking separation from existing nation-states. Militant Islamic groups with local ambitions have adopted terrorist tactics in Algeria, Egypt, Lebanon, Palestine, Pakistan, Kashmir,

Afghanistan, Saudi Arabia, Dubai and several other places. Drawing Islamists engaged in such local actions into a broader transnational network is an objective that al-Qaeda and related groups have pursued with some success. Groups with many other kinds of entrenched political and moral agendas have given rise to episodes of terrorist action. They include, for example, white supremacists and right-wing militias in the US; left-wing militants in Italy, Germany and Colombia; and rural movements in Peru and Uganda. Add to them Haganah, Irgun and the Stern Gang (Lehi) with their different agendas for the creation of Israel, and EOKA (Ethnikí Orgánosis Kipriakoú Agónos) supporting union of Cyprus with Greece, and the full spectrum of terrorist organizations becomes more evident.

Why are terrorist attacks so rare?

Anyone who thinks about the possibility of a terrorist attack senses how vulnerable we are in public places, work sites and even at home. Full protection is simply out of reach. For people with a driving motive, without inhibitions against killing civilians and without faith in other avenues of action, the temptation must be great to launch threats and attacks.

But in fact group terrorism is relatively rare and even the most deadly and disruptive episodes destroy lives and structures in quite small areas compared to the more highly organized and equipped destruction accomplished by armed forces. Statistically, terrorism is well down on the list of the dangers humans face. Later we will consider why the danger of terrorism receives so much attention despite its rarity, but here the question is: why have group terrorist attacks been so rare?

Terrorism rarely achieves its goals. Part of the answer lies in the fact that much of the time terrorist acts fail to advance the objectives their perpetrators

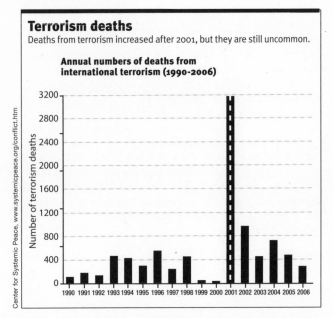

Terrorism deaths

Deaths from terrorism increased after 2001, but they are still uncommon.

**Annual numbers of deaths from
international terrorism (1990-2006)**

Center for Systemic Peace, www.systemicpeace.org/conflict.htm

seek. Those who engage in terrorism usually intend more than murder and mayhem; they seek to alter governments and to change policies. Creating localized mayhem is relatively easy, but under most conditions the probability of gaining a political objective through terrorist acts is small. Governments rarely change policy in response to terrorism, or not in the direction that terrorists desire. Instead they resist, often ferociously, in part because they tend to think the terrorists intended not to provoke a change of policy but to hurt and kill innocent people and to cause mayhem. People who decide to commit terrorism have to convince themselves that their case is different. Often people sympathetic to the same political cause will reject terrorism on practical grounds.

Terrorism has most reliably succeeded where the terrorist group, in addition to targeting civilians, conducts guerrilla war against military and police units and where the government under attack has already lost legitimacy in the eyes of the people it governs. The most striking examples are nationalist movements against colonialism or separatist movements seeking control of territory, some of which were noted above. Once colonial powers recognized they could no longer hold their empires, their departure was often accelerated by violence or threats of violence.[8]

State terrorism appears to have more chance of successful outcomes than group terrorism does. Its greater effectiveness is one reason it is more widespread than group terrorism. State terrorism by proxy (using or creating terrorist groups to operate against the government of another country) has the same strategic weaknesses as group terrorism, but if the aim is

Risk comparison: fatalities from terrorism and other causes

Global terrorism fatalities in recent years (including Iraq)

1998	2,172	2003	2,349
1999	864	2004	5,066
2000	783	2005	8,194
2001	4,571	2006	12,070
2002	2,763		

Some other causes of death globally in year 2000

Road traffic	1,259,838
Self-inflicted injury	814,778
Interpersonal violence of people 15-44 years	335,202
War injuries of people 15-44 years	167,329

Some causes of death in the US per year for 2003/2006

Speeding related auto crashes	13,100 to 13,400
Dog bites	15 to 25
Terrorist attacks	0 to 3

MIPT Terrorism Knowledge Base, www.tkb.org/Home.jsp; M Peden, K McGee and E Krug, (eds.), *Injury: A Leading Cause of the Global Burden of Disease*, 2000, World Health Organization, Geneva, 2002, http://whqlibdoc.who.int/publications/2002/9241562323.pdf; National Highway Traffic Safety Administration, www-nrd.nhtsa.dot.gov/departments/nrd-30/ncsa/AvailInf.html; K Phillips, Dog Bite Law website, www.dogbitelaw.com

Activists against terrorism

Palestine 2002: We the undersigned feel that it is our national responsibility to issue this appeal in light of the dangerous situation engulfing the Palestinian people. We call upon the parties behind military operations targeting civilians in Israel to reconsider their policies and stop driving our young men to carry out these operations. Suicide bombings deepen the hatred and widen the gap between the Palestinian and Israeli people. Also, they destroy the possibilities of peaceful co-existence between them in two neighboring states.

We see that these bombings do not contribute towards achieving our national project that calls for freedom and independence. On the contrary, they strengthen the enemies of peace on the Israeli side and give Israel's aggressive government under Sharon the excuse to continue its harsh war against our people. This war targets our children, elderly, villages, cities, and our national hopes and achievements.
Signatories:
Dr Sari Nusseibeh, Dr Hanan Ashrawi and many other Palestinian intellectuals and public figures.

As printed in *Al-Quds* newspaper, Jerusalem, 20 June 2002 and in many other places.

Russia 1916: At all events, we are convinced that the experience of revolution and counter-revolution in Russia has proved the correctness of our Party's more than twenty-year struggle against terrorism as tactics. We must not forget, however, that ... [we] have always stood for the use of violence in the mass struggle... Secondly, we linked the struggle against terrorism with many years of propaganda ... for an armed uprising... as the best means by which the proletariat can retaliate to the government's policy... [and] as the inevitable result of the development of the class struggle for socialism and democracy. Thirdly, we have... supported the use of violence by the masses against their oppressors, particularly in street demonstrations... and systematic mass resistance against the police and the army... inducing the peasantry and the army to take a conscious part in this struggle. These are the tactics we have applied in the struggle against terrorism, and it is our firm conviction that they have proved successful.

VI Lenin, Speech at the Congress of the Social-Democratic Party of Switzerland, 4 November 1916. From VI Lenin, *Collected Works*, 4th English Edition, Ed MS Levin, Progress Publishers, Moscow, 1964, Vol 23.

to implant endemic conflict in another country in order to weaken it, even at the cost of much painful violence and economic disruption, then terrorism by proxy looks quite effective. That seems to have been the intent of the US in sponsoring the Contras in Nicaragua in the 1980s and of Rhodesia and South Africa in creating Renamo in Mozambique in 1975 and supporting it through the 1980s, all in the name of thwarting communist expansion. State terrorism against a country's own population also seems to have a better chance of success than group terrorism does. Making people fearful and passive, eliminating active opponents, ethnic cleansing, and genocide have been achieved by terrorist regimes. Creating positive legitimacy by means of state terrorism has been much more elusive, however.

Moral and legal barriers. According to all ordinary moral codes terrorist acts are wrong. Strong social controls and moral strictures work against terrorist acts. To destroy private or public property is already to step beyond the limit of normal morality and the law; threatening and killing people is a much worse crime. Activists who turn to violence to pursue political objectives are often reluctant to target civilians. All major religions teach that killing is rarely justified and the moral codes of almost all families and friendship groups frown on murder. All the social pressures and powers of law enforcement that discourage other kinds of crime also work against terrorism. The pressures are physical as well as moral: suspected terrorists are often arrested, tried and punished. They are likely to suffer long detentions, tough questioning (often torture) and severe punishment, including death.

The moral code against attacking, injuring and killing civilians also works against the use of terrorism as 'propaganda of the deed' in an effort to shape public opinion. The public is likely to be more deeply repelled by the shedding of blood than impressed by the urgency of the terrorist cause.

State terrorism may have an easier time finding a moral and legal defense than does group terrorism. Governments are recognized to have a moral license to employ violence if it is done lawfully. For them it is no great stretch to lend the veneer of law to transgressions against the rights of citizens, to authorize extra-legal actions or to claim executive discretion in security matters. Moreover, defense of the state in the lawless terrain of international tensions can be used to justify all kinds of interventions.

Lack of material support. To sustain a move to violent action that might include terrorism, a group needs material support as well as a moral justification. Although the budget for a basic terrorist operation is not large, it takes effort, money and skill to assemble arms, training and ways of organizing. The Central Intelligence Agency (CIA) estimates that prior to 2001 al-Qaeda had an annual budget of about $30 million. That would put it at the level of the military spending of small states like Jamaica, Togo, or Djibouti. It had several training camps in Sudan, Afghanistan, Philippines and Indonesia at various times with buildings, computers, satellite telephones, weapons, munitions, rudimentary laboratories and medical facilities. That it had access to a large financial flow from wealthy Saudi donors and far-flung charity organizations has been widely reported. It could buy airplane tickets, pay training fees and cover the living expenses of members of many associated cells operating in expensive cities in Spain, Germany, France, Belgium, Netherlands, Italy, Britain, and the US and also in less expensive countries like Pakistan.

At the other end of the spectrum, it took the five Canadian activists who called themselves 'Direct Action' more than a year in the early 1980s to steal the necessary weapons, explosives and cash; do research on targets; design and build timing devices;

and train themselves in handling arms before they were able to plant their first bomb at Dunsmuir electrical power station on Vancouver Island in order to stop a power line that they believed would serve pulp and paper company owners and harm the environment and native people. They took care not to harm workers and hoped to stiffen the resolve of peace and environmental groups. But another action meant to expose and punish Canada's arms business went off the track when their truck bomb at the Litton Industries plant in Toronto that made guidance systems for cruise missiles injured 10 people.[9]

In the days of Cold War antagonism, groups could often gain support from governments on one side or the other, and sometimes from both. Today, governments, large ones projecting power globally and small ones interested in destabilizing a hostile neighbor, are still the most important source of material support for most terrorist groups. Other sources are business interests; clandestine trade in drugs, diamonds and similar goods that are easy to smuggle; crimes such as kidnapping, theft and credit card fraud; and remittances from supporters, often members of diaspora communities that identify with a cause. Not infrequently the flow of income becomes a sustaining motive as well as a helpful means for perpetuating a group with terrorist potential.

Hard to justify. Despite all the barriers groups do undertake terrorism, sometimes on a large scale, as the case of the Liberation Tigers of Tamil Eelam (LTTE) shows. In their fight to carve an independent Tamil state out of the northern part of Sri Lanka they have created an effective guerrilla army and resisted attacks by the Sri Lankan and Indian armies. The LTTE has also directed hundreds of terrorist actions against government and military leaders, moderate Tamil politicians, rival Tamil guerrilla leaders, leaders of the Muslim minority, and economic facilities staffed with workers and surrounded by crowds. They may have invented the suicide bomb vest and their 200 to 240 suicide bombings since 1983 can claim some spectacular results, including the murder of Prime Minister Rajiv Gandhi of India in 1991 and President Ranasinghe Premadasa of Sri Lanka in 1993.

A statement of the president of the LTTE illustrates the problem faced by anyone attempting publicly to justify terrorism. Velupillai Prabhakaran claimed in a speech on 27 November 2001 that groups like his were not terrorist because they used violence 'for a concrete political objective'. The global battle against terrorism, he asserted, should target 'real terrorists.'[10] Six bloody years later, after a ceasefire had failed and large-scale fighting and frequent terror attacks had resumed, Prabhakaran made the same claim that LTTE violence was rationally designed to win freedom for the Tamil homeland. He was on stronger ground when he accused the political and military leaders of Sri Lanka of terrorizing and killing Tamil civilians with bombing raids and of seeking a military solution to 'the Tamil national question'.[11] Yet it is hard to deny that LTTE terrorism, far from winning independence for the Tamil homeland, contributes to the intransigence, chauvinism and militarism on the Sinhalese side of the conflict.

In addition to claiming a just struggle, defenders of terrorism (who may not use that term) make several other arguments. They note the absence of other means of action and claim that the people attacked are not really civilians (they are soldiers since they support a government or an army engaged in repression) or that they are criminals and murderers. They even suggest that the people they target are not fully human; they are savage, uncivilized, monstrous, irreligious or evil and not entitled to full human rights. Some groups accused of terrorism deny that they target civilians, or even people, at all. They aim to destroy machinery (logging equipment), facilities (bank offices), weapons (fighter planes), documents (military draft records), or symbols (flags) that embody or represent the forces they oppose. Injury to people for these activists is not terrorism; it is a technical error, what governments call 'collateral damage' when they seek to justify attacks that harm civilians during wars and in counter-terrorist campaigns.

Recruitment

Because terrorist acts are hard to justify in moral and practical terms, recruiters of future terrorists are often faced with a difficult task. Several kinds of justification have to work together in a receptive environment before many people will join a group committing acts of terrorism. We will explore some of the features of a receptive environment in chapter five. It is sufficient here to note that the appeal of engaging in terrorism is undoubtedly greater for people who feel that they have been humiliated, disempowered and disadvantaged and who see no alternative to a violent course of action. The story is similar to that of youth who join violent gangs and armies. The attraction is an emotional as well as an intellectual process. The particular causes are of many kinds, but a successful appeal often takes the form of a broad, symbolic and impassioned call from a revered leader to a pre-existing group of friends or associates. The call is often to pursue a trans-historical ideal, whether it be a new nation, a political religion, a classless society or something else against the forces of an intransigent enemy. Group solidarity reinforces the justification by making participation in terrorist acts a sacred gesture of solidarity.

Alternatives often exist. Given the statistical, moral, legal and physical disincentives, it is not surprising that most political activists choose other avenues of action, from contesting elections and organizing strikes to mounting mass demonstrations and going on hunger campaigns. Where governments have closed off other channels of action, aggrieved people may find violent action the best alternative, but even then many will prefer to attack police posts, government offices and army camps rather than to target civilians.

Fear of failure. Once all the other inhibitions have been overcome, would-be terrorists have to consider the chances that the attack itself will fail or hit the wrong target, or that they will be caught before they can act. The consequences could be morally and physically painful and humiliating. There are many cases of suicide bombers who did not ignite their explosives and were captured. There is no way of knowing how many planned attacks are canceled or aborted out of fear of failure.

The brief tour of weapons, opportunities and motives suggests that some terrorism will always occur at the edge of politics. Political order and loyalty extend only so far. A political grievance, an experience of oppression or neglect, a failure of security, or a religious revival will push some people over the edge to a place where the rules of civic security no longer apply. To know that terrorism is always possible leaves unanswered the question of why it flares up and persists in certain times and places. Nor does it explain whether terrorism now is or is not a prominent danger that should preoccupy governments and citizens alike. A brief account of some examples of religious, nationalist and political terrorist episodes will help to clarify how to approach these questions.

Religious militants

Several of the most active and persistent bouts of terrorism in recent times are connected with religion. Some militant Christians, Sikhs, Muslims, Hindus, Jews and adherents of other religions have built their action on the conviction that their religious calling requires violent defense against its enemies. Where most of us see terrorism against innocent civilians, some of the religious militants see a just war against agents of evil.

The large majority of the adherents of the major religions that have produced terrorist offshoots do not support terrorism. Many are content to practice their faith under a government that protects the right to practice any faith or no faith. Others stand behind political action to boost the voice of their religion in politics and even to put in place a government that will rule according to the precepts and prescriptions of their faith, but they draw the line at violence. Still others might support guerrilla war against military targets and institutions of domination and control, but not terrorist violence against civilians. The militants who believe their religion demands terrorist actions always face two sets of enemies: those outside the religion and the co-religionists, usually the majority, who oppose the use of terror. Both have become targets of terrorist acts.

Right wingers who commit terrorist acts in the US often cite their reading of Christian doctrine as justification for their action. The Army of God affirms the legitimacy of using force 'to defend the life of an unborn child'. Reverend Michael Bray served four years in prison for destroying seven abortion clinics in the region around Washington DC in the 1980s. His book, *A Time to Kill*, advocates the use against abortionists of 'defensive force,' a euphemism for assassination.[12] He advocates a version of Dominion Theology with its belief that Christians are called to bring all societies under the rule of God's Word.

Another doctrine, Christian Identity, believes in a coming revolution led by European whites, the true descendents of the tribes of Israel, that will overthrow the evil and duplicitous Zionist Occupation Government (they call it 'ZOG') and establish a racially-pure society governed by biblical laws. It teaches that Jews are the offspring of Satan and that non-whites have an inferior origin as 'mud people.' It supplies the religious side of the thinking of the patriot movement, militias and several white supremacy groups. Adherents are responsible for many racially motivated attacks on non-whites, mixed-race couples, and immigrants.[13]

Public revulsion after the Oklahoma City bombing in 1995 and penetration of groups by the Federal Bureau of Investigation (FBI) contributed to a weakening of rightwing organizations in the US. The attacks of 11 September 2001 added to the disarray as some rightwing leaders applauded the attacks on the 'Jewish towers,' some opposed the growing government security apparatus, and others rallied to a military response against non-white foreigners.[14]

Islamic renewal

Islam, like Christianity, boasts a large number of differing doctrines competing for attention and adherents. The leading ideas for renewing the political expression of Islam came after World War Two from activists in Egypt and Pakistan who opposed the trend to secular nationalism. In Egypt in the 1950s and 1960s President Abdel Gamal Nasser came down hard on Muslim writers and activists like Hasan al-Banna who founded the Muslim Brotherhood, and Sayyid Qutb, an influential writer and leading advocate of a purified Islam. They and Mawlana Mawdudi, founder in Pakistan of Jamaat-i-Islami (Islamic Assembly), wanted the Muslim world to gain the advantages of science and technical change on its own terms within a state organized to reflect the teachings of Islam.

For these activists the founding of Israel, the millions of Palestinian refugees and the unemployment and poverty of Muslim societies were so many indications of the failure of secular nationalism in the Middle East and the Muslim world. For Mawdudi, the threat to

Muslim identity and to pan-Islamic unity brought by British and French colonialism was perpetuated in the secular nationalism promoted by leaders like Gandhi and Nehru in India, Sukarno in Indonesia and Nasser in Egypt.

Qutb and Mawdudi developed an activist ideology with a specific form of Islam as the all-inclusive guide for individuals and countries facing change and disruption. They taught that the Qur'an, the example of Muhammad's own life and the early Muslim community are the models to follow. Islamic law is the template for Muslim political structures. Social revolution and scientific progress must be pursued within Islam and not by borrowing Western ideas and values. To construct a true Islamic society means engaging in a personal and a political struggle or jihad for true Islam in an environment polluted by ignorance, greed and immorality, a condition Qutb termed 'jahiliyya'. Muslim governments that fail to implement sharia law and true Islam are as much a part of jahiliyya as the Western societies that have defiled Islam from the time of the crusades.[15]

In the late 1960s and the 1970s several leaders and associations dedicated to Islamic reform in Egypt, Lebanon and Palestine reinforced the tendency to use violence against their governments, accusing them of betraying Islam. Their critique of the ruling groups became more bitter and their actions more violent after the debacle of the 1967 Arab-Israeli war and Arab loss of land and dignity.

The internationalist version of the movement for a purified Islam received a great boost after 1979. The US and the West, along with Saudi Arabia, were among the main boosters. Pervez Amir Ali Hoodbhoy explains: 'With Pakistan's Mohammed Zia ul-Haq as America's foremost ally, the CIA openly recruited Islamic holy warriors from Egypt, Saudi Arabia, Sudan and Algeria. Radical Islam went into overdrive as its superpower ally and mentor funneled support to the mujaheddin; Ronald Reagan feted them on the White House lawn.' The Saudi Government and Pakistan's Interservice Intelligence Agency (ISI) collaborated in the project. The US saw a double payoff. Thwarting the Soviets in Afghanistan was as attractive as diverting militant Islam away from the Middle East.[17]

The withdrawal of the Soviets from Afghanistan in February 1989 was a dramatic turning point. What appeared to be an unalloyed victory for the US-Saudi strategy of diverting and controlling the new energies of militant Islam was in reality the beginning of a newly transnational terrorist force. There was, as well, an explosion of new Islamic organizations and movements in other countries that fed on the impatience of urban youth, many of them poor, for the jobs and material benefits that existing governments had failed to deliver. Two examples: During the Intifada that began in 1987 in Palestine, Hamas, with its social service branches and its hardline opposition to Israel, became a powerful rival to Yasser Arafat's secular Palestine Liberation Organization (PLO). In the early 1990s in Algeria, the Islamic Salvation Front mounted a strong political and electoral challenge to the nationalist government. Only a military coup and a wrenching civil war kept it from power.

The experience of the tens of thousands of Muslim youth from a dozen countries who studied and trained to fight in Afghanistan reinforced an internationalist current in the new activism. Although the ideas that guided the formation of the camps were derived from the tradition of Qutb and Mawdudi as well as Saudi Arabia's version of purified Islam, Wahhabism, the training seems to have been much more limited and quite instrumental, aimed at creating a loyal, unquestioning and effective force committed to fight against both the corrupted governments of the Islamic world and the centers of global dominance in the US and Europe. The multinational experience of training, fighting and winning made it possible for certain ambitious militant leaders to imagine new kinds of attacks on the forces of evil and to find people willing and able to carry them out. How the new global ambitions and still potent local forces have shaped the pattern of Islamist terrorism since 11 September 2001 is a major theme of chapter five.

Nationalists without a state

Nationalism, like religion, can rouse intense political passions. The transformation of empires into nation-states, first in Europe and then in Europe's colonial empires, inaugurated a long period of political turmoil, often marked by blood and terror. The question of which group's cultural identity will gain political expression is still hotly contested in many places.

Governments almost always resist dismemberment. Sometimes the experience or threat of violence results in the division of one country into two (Bangladesh broke away from Pakistan in 1971 in a punishing war in which India also took part), sometimes with a confirming referendum (Eritrea became independent of Ethiopia in 1993 also after a long war). More commonly the thwarted nationalists will be offered a measure of autonomy short of independence in a bid to transmute a conflict headed for violence into a political process, but committed nationalists may continue to dream of full sovereignty. Violence has always been a prime means of state formation. Since the Second World War nationalist struggles have tended to take the form of guerrilla warfare, but terrorism is an ever-present possibility that sometimes becomes an important, even defining, element in the struggle.

Western Europe and North America, despite their relatively old and well-established nation-states, harbor several unresolved nationalist claims. The movements that have made the greatest use of violence against civilians are the Irish Republican Army (IRA) and Basque Homeland and Liberty (*Euzkadi Ta Azkatasunaor*, ETA). Other movements like the Front de Libération de Quebec (FLQ) and the National Liberation Front of Corsica (FLNC) have resorted to terrorism from time to time.

The case of Basque Homeland and Liberty (ETA) illustrates how nationalist terrorism comes about. ETA grew out of the Basque Nationalist Party that since 1894 had stood for preserving and increasing the legal autonomy that the Basque region of Spain and France had retained since the Middle Ages. The nationalists suffered heavy repression under Franco's authoritarian and centralizing rule. Basque autonomy was abolished and the nationalist leadership went into exile in Paris. When political demonstrations and other non-violent action produced no gains, a group of younger nationalists in 1959 founded ETA with the intention of using the tactics of anti-colonial nationalist movements to win Basque independence. As long as ETA was fighting Spain's fascist government the use of violence had much support in the Basque region and from democrats in other regions of Spain and in other countries. That did not prevent the organization from splitting into nationalist and revolutionary socialist wings with the revolutionaries more willing to use sabotage and assassination as tactics of struggle. Their main targets were government officials, politicians and military forces.

In a dramatic action in 1973 ETA assassinated Franco's presumed successor, Admiral Luis Carrero Blanco. Their action probably hastened the end of the fascist dictatorship. It also initiated what ETA calls the 'action-reprisal-action' cycle. The regime sent in the troops to punish the perpetrators and set off a lengthy regional war. A decade of active terrorism ensued. In 1980, their bloodiest year, ETA killed 118 people. One response was terrorist attacks on ETA members for several years in the 1980s by a group with ties to the Government of Spain, the *Grupos Antiterroristas de Liberación* (GAL). The reciprocal use of terrorism was a severe challenge for the recently established democratic constitution of the country. Once the Basque region was accorded some autonomy, ETA's policy lost public support in its home region and became disputed within the movement, but a core of die-hard fighters for independence refused offers of amnesty and eluded arrest.

Spain and ETA

Influenced by the experience of the Irish Republican Army, ETA declared a ceasefire in September 1998 and called upon the political wing of Basque nationalism to negotiate self-determination. By then they had killed almost 800 people, more than half of them Spanish soldiers and police. The Spanish Government continued making arrests and ETA proceeded with attacks against property and raids on arms depots. After little more than a year ETA declared the peace process 'blocked and poisoned' and announced that after 3 December 1999 it would 'reactivate the armed struggle.' A strong movement to end the violence developed in the Basque region and the rest of Spain. For a time, each attack provoked a counter demonstration. For example, on 2 March 2002 organizers said that 50,000 demonstrators marched in the Basque coastal town of Portugalete to protest an attack that injured socialist politician Esther Cabezudo and her bodyguard Enrique Torres. In 2003 the Government banned the Basque nationalist political party, Batasuna, as a political organization for channeling funds to ETA.

For a while it seemed that the shocks of the attacks of 11 September 2001 in the US and of 11 March 2004 in Madrid might open the antagonists to a negotiated solution. In June 2004 and again in March 2006 ETA announced ceasefires, but successful talks did not follow, arrests continued and the attacks resumed. In November 2007, in the run-up to elections, the governing Socialist Party and the opposition Popular Party are both took a hard line against ETA and Batasuna, both of which had been weakened by arrests.[18]

At the heart of the idea of the nation-state is found an irreducible ambiguity. The globe's almost 200 states are far from reflecting all the cultural groups that express a national political calling. Oppressed and unrecognized cultures continue to voice political aspirations, and sometimes splinter off groups that engage in terrorism in the name of their claim: Kurds in Turkey, Iran and Iraq; Sikhs in India; Aceh in Indonesia; Albanians in Kosovo and many others.

Movements of the Left and Right

The goal of groups moved by political ideology is to change the institutions and policies of government and to put new kinds of people in power. Disputes between dissidents and governments on such matters is the stuff of normal political conflict, but oppositional groups sometimes choose to employ terror in addition to or instead of other forms of action. During the Cold War, groups in several Western capitalist countries adopted sabotage, assassination and bombings as forms of action.

Italy in the 1960s and 1970s, for example, experienced an especially active period of violence sometimes called 'the years of lead' with many attacks by rightwing and leftwing groups. Its impact reached a peak on March 16, 1978 when members of Italy's Red Brigades kidnapped and murdered Aldo Moro, leader of the Christian Democratic Party and five-time premier of Italy. They chose the day of the 'historic compromise' between the Christian Democrats and the Italian Communist Party (PCI), an arrangement avidly opposed by the Red Brigades who saw themselves as true followers of revolutionary Maxism-Leninism at a time when the PCI had joined the mainstream. Founded in Milan in 1970 by Renato Curcio and Margherita Cagol, the Red Brigades grew out of a Marxist study group at the University of Trento. Their violence started with firebombing industrial targets and then expanded to kidnapping, kneecapping and, finally, murder. Terrorist acts continued into the 1980s, including the bombing of Bologna's central rail station in August 1980 by the neo-fascist *Nuclei Armati Rivoluzionari* (NAR), killing 85 and injuring more than 200. Between 1970 and 1982 the Red Brigades claimed responsibility for over 2000 illegal acts in which 161 people were killed.

The Red Brigades were only the most enduring of many similar organizations: 537 differently named groups with some continuity of existence have been counted in Italy during those years. Another 199 people were killed in terrorist acts not claimed by the Red Brigades. In the mid 1980s the Red Brigades were fading. Arrests, internal divisions, defections via amnesty and ideological crisis weakened them. In 1984 four leaders in prison published a letter abandoning armed struggle: 'The international conditions that made this struggle possible no longer exist.'[19]

The Red Brigades are an example of leftwing terrorism that fit the ideological contestation of the Cold War. Other examples include the Red Army Faction (often called the Baader-Meinhoff Gang) in Germany, the Weather Underground in the United States and Direct Action in Canada. The latter two tried to confine their violence to property and many of their members would deny that they were terrorists. Although these organizations identified with the Marxist left, they broke from the old-left idea that action must be based on an analysis of class forces and on organized support from the working class. What the old left saw as avoiding premature 'voluntarism' looked to the new revolutionaries as a failure of nerve when social conditions demanded action.

Groups with racist, anti-immigrant and anti-government ideologies are numerous and active in Europe and North America. Notable in the United States has been the right wing terrorism of white supremacist groups like the Ku Klux Klan and Aryan Nation and populist armed militias, convinced that Jewish-communist-capitalists have turned the Federal Government and the UN into engines of oppression. Their ideology overlaps with Christian groups that oppose the existing non-believing institutions and dream of authority guided by the true faith. In Europe rightwing groups are investigated as extremist, rather than terrorist, but several members of Blood and Honor, a neo-Nazi organization, were arrested in connection with terrorist acts in Poland and Belgium in 2006.[20] Targets of rightwing attacks include synagogues, mosques, churches, inter-racial couples, Muslims, Jews, abortion-providers, immigrants, Roma people and gay men. The targets differ from country to country, but Russia, India, Hungary, Britain and the US have seen numerous attacks.

Groups that have engaged in rightwing terror have sometimes been closely connected with the government or with the military, as the next chapter will discuss. Leftwing terrorism has declined over the past four decades. Governments had some success in penetrating organizations to learn their plans and in arresting key members. With the end of the Soviet Union a major source of inspiration and support for anti-capitalist causes dried up and the victory of the last anti-colonial struggles changed militants into politicians and administrators. Left-wing political thought no longer claimed a scientific social analysis from which to derive a clear-cut strategy of social revolution. Some of the remaining movements, like the Revolutionary Armed Forces of Colombia (FARC), are still powerful, but they look more and more like political gangs interested in preserving their piece of power. Others, like Revolutionary Struggle in Greece, seem propelled by broadly anti-capitalist or anarchist ideas applied to domestic politics. Some observers fear that anti-globalization activism and the environmental movement will give rise to terrorist attacks, but there is no indication of any trend in that direction.

How dangerous?

Criminologists have discovered that the level of fear of crime in a society is not very closely related to the actual danger of being a victim of crime. Fear of terrorism is similar: it moves up and down in response to political pronouncements and striking incidents as well as in response to changes in the actual incidence of terrorist acts.

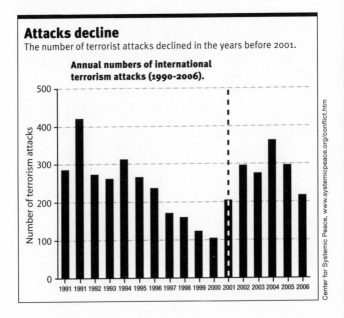

Attacks decline
The number of terrorist attacks declined in the years before 2001.

Annual numbers of international terrorism attacks (1990-2006).

Center for Systemic Peace, www.systemicpeace.org/conflict.htm

Dangers and fears

Before the attacks of 11 September 2001, the trackers of terrorism in the US State Department identified two distinct trends: a long-term decline since 1987 in the number of terrorist incidents worldwide and rising destructiveness of the attacks that were committed.[21] The public in the US ranked terrorism rather low in a universe of terrible dangers that also included war, natural disaster, ecological breakdown, economic depression and epidemics. The public in other regions, including Europe, also seemed to have learned to live with a level of terrorism, which in most places was declining, without giving the matter much thought. For people in regions especially afflicted by political violence like Israel, Palestine, Colombia and Sri Lanka the issue, of course, remained an urgent concern.

Since the attacks in New York and Washington, Bali, Madrid and London, and the ongoing theme of terrorist violence in Afghanistan and Iraq, there has been a concerted effort to keep terrorism at the top of the political agenda. But is the danger really rising? Government officials and think-tank experts believe that terrorist networks are organizing globally and that the sophistication of their communication, planning, training and recruitment has also increased. Moreover, terrorist groups that formerly had localized objectives such as replacing the government in Egypt, Saudi Arabia or Indonesia, join together in al-Qaeda and add to their separate aims the global goal of damaging the power of the US and its supporters.

The experts also say the failure of several post-colonial nation-states to bring order to their territory creates physical and social spaces where terrorists can gather, organize, perfect and teach their techniques and their ideology. Furthermore, bombs and guns are more powerful than they were a few years ago and the underground makers of weapons have better technical skills. It is also possible that available civilian technology could be turned into a weapon of unprecedented lethal capacity by, for example, crashing an airplane into a nuclear electricity generating plant. Recently the experts have signaled a huge jump in danger; they point out that it is now technically possible for terrorist groups to initiate a smallpox epidemic, poison the water or the food supply of a large population or explode a device that spreads radiation in a metropolis. The point is made repeatedly: nuclear, biological or chemical weapons and transnational terrorist networks that make the global power of the US and Europe their prime enemy are reasons for Western governments to take terrorism much more seriously.

Some important facts support these assessments, but the question of the danger of terrorism is caught in the dilemma of prophesies that may be self-fulfilling. A more lethal arsenal does create new orders of danger, and the technical, organizational and financial skill of terrorist groups is impressive. But in order to assess the danger of terrorism properly it must be recognized that the problem does not reside solely with the terrorist groups. They and the governments they attack are part of a larger pattern. The advances in explosives and other weapons are not made by terrorists, they are the work of weapons laboratories financed by governments.

The financial circuits that terrorists use are an aspect of globalizing business relations. Often groups that are now terrorists got a significant boost earlier in their trajectory from a government agency of some kind, as the Taliban and al-Qaeda did from the US, Pakistan and Saudi Arabia. In any particular case the actions and policies of the governments under terrorist threat are part of the motivational dynamic. One may ask, for example, whether Western powers have contributed to state breakdown and popular anger that has found expression in terrorist ideologies? In what measure has President Bush's war on terror and the invasions of Afghanistan and Iraq generated a widening terrorist response, created a training ground for future terrorists and raised the status of terrorists from that of criminals preying on civilian innocents to that of warriors in a global cause? Finally, do not repeated reminders that security is at risk, and that there is reason to fear, feed the sense of self-importance of would-be terrorists? After taking a closer look at state terrorism and counter-terrorism we will be in a better position to address these questions.

1 *Time*, 11 March 2002. **2** John Roth, Douglas Greenburg and Serena Wille, 'Appendix A: The Financing of the 9/11 Plot', Staff report to the Commission in Monograph on Terrorist Financing, National Commission on Terrorist Attacks upon the United States, 2004. **3** Lloyd Dixon and Rachel Kaganoff Stern, Compensation for Losses from the 9/11 Attacks, RAND, 2004. **4** Glen Hodgson, The Economic Cost of Terrorism, Export Development Canada, 2004. **5** Brian Whittaker, *The Guardian*, 4 March 2002. **6** Richard Wike, 'Widespread Negativity: Muslims Distrust Westerners More Than Vice Versa', senior researcher Richard Wike, Pew Research Center, Pew Global Attitudes Project, 2007, www.pewglobal.org. **7** 'Muslim Public Opinion on US Policy, Attacks on Civilians and al-Qaeda', principal investigator Steven Kull, The Program on International Policy Attitudes at the University of Maryland, 2007. **8** Max Abrahms, 'Why Terrorism Does Not Work', International Security 31, no 2, Fall 2006: 42–78. **9** Ann Hansen, Direct Action: Memoirs of an Urban Guerrilla, Between the Lines, 2001. **10** *The Hindu*, 27 November 2001. **11** Tamil Eelam national leader in his annual Heroes' Day statement, 27 November 2007, official website of the Peace Secretariat of the LTTE, www.ltteps.org. **12** Michael Bray, *A Time to Kill: A Study Concerning the Use of Force and Abortion*, Advocates for Life, 1993. **13** Southern Poverty Law Center: www.splcenter.org. **14** Martin Durham, 'The American Far Right and 9/11', Terrorism and Political Violence 15, no 2, Summer 2003: 96–111. **15** John L Esposito, Unholy War: Terror in the Name of Islam, Oxford University Press, 2002. **16** Pervez Amir Ali Hoodbhoy, 'How Islam Lost Its Way', The Washington Post, 30 December 2001. **17** Gilles Kepel, 'The Trail of Political Islam', OpenDemocracy.Net, 3 July 2002, www.opendemocracy.net/forum **18** Paddy Woodworth, 'The Spanish-Basque Peace Process: How to Get Things Wrong', World Policy Journal, Spring 2007, 1–9. **19** Quoted by the International Policy Institute for Counter-Terrorism at www.ict.org.il **20** Europol, TE-SAT 2007: EU Terrorism Situation and Trend Report 2007, Max-Peter Ratzel, Director of Europol, Europol Corporate Communications 2007. **21** US State Department, Patterns of Global Terrorism 2001. Released by the Office of the Coordinator for Counter-terrorism, 21 May 2002, www.state.gov

3 State terrorism

Terrorism always lurks at the back of the shelf of power tools available to those who command the machinery of government. The agencies and weapons that pursue criminals and wage wars are easily adapted to state-terrorist use. Whether coping with internal opposition or projecting power abroad, holders of state power have frequently chosen terrorism as one of their instruments of action.

STATE TERRORISM HAS an ancient history, but its modern expression is tied to the projection of European state power in acquiring empires in America, Asia and Africa. Spain, Portugal, the Netherlands, Britain, France, Germany, Italy and Japan all used force with frightening moral certainty when they established empires. So did the United States in its westward expansion and Russia in its eastward extension. These wars of expansion often included attacks on civilians. One of the first examples of biological terrorism was the deliberate distribution of smallpox-infected blankets to North American Indians.[1]

In places of European settlement, as in the Americas and Southern Africa, the indigenous people who resisted the invaders also attacked the new homesteads and settlements. The new settlers, who considered themselves ordinary citizens, appeared to indigenous people as armed thieves threatening their land and game. Fear of such attacks reinforced the military and political drive to clear indigenous people from ancestral lands and either exterminate them or confine them to officially designated reservations.

The colonial powers continued to use violence to maintain their domination, to recruit labor and soldiers and to seize additional territory for settler farms, mines and other uses. In opening new lands to commercial exploitation colonial governments often

Colonial terror

The British [sent] search-and-destroy missions... to Central India in 1817 to slaughter the marauding Pindari armies of Chitu... Colonel George Fitzclarence, an aide-de-camp to the Governor of Bengal... underlined their real purpose. The Pindaris were 'viewed as public robbers', Fitzclarence wrote, and so 'their extirpation was aimed at, and not their defeat as an enemy entitled to the rights of war.'

[There was a] prolonged campaign to exterminate the San (Bushmen) during the first decades of the 19th century. Hundreds of thousands of acres were seized by white farmers, and hardly a single Bushman band remained by 1825. A correspondent in a frontier town in 1821, describing how he had met people involved in the 'commando' expeditions sent out against them, wrote that 'they talk of shooting Bushmen with the same feelings as if the poor creatures were wild beasts.'

Colonel William Cox [a wealthy Australian rancher], speaking at a public meeting in Beaufort in 1825: 'The best thing that could be done would be to shoot all the Blacks and manure the ground with their carcasses, which was all the good they were fit for... the women and children should especially be shot as the most certain method of getting rid of the race.'

Richard Gott 'Shoot them to be sure', *London Review of Books*, 25 April 2002.

ceded political control to private companies. Some of the worst episodes of terror were carried out under the direction of such companies to further their collection of natural resources. The forced gathering of wild rubber in King Leopold's Congo rivaled in its destructiveness the depredations of the slave trade. Profits from wild rubber were also the incentive for the systematic use of terror to recruit and discipline labor in the forests of the Amazon basin.

Once colonial governments were in place and colonial armies had put down most rebellions, the use of terror decreased but it did not disappear. Senegalese movie director Ousmane Sembene's film *Emitai* (1971) depicts a historical incident in the French campaign to recruit soldiers and confiscate grain in West African villages for the French war effort in Europe during

World War Two. The women hide the rice and the young men hide in the backlands. The drama descends inevitably into the massacre by colonial police of villagers trying to keep their freedom and conserve their food supply. A few conscience-stricken colonial officials have no way to interrupt the train of events; they are anguished, but implicated. Violence and the threat of violence against civilians who resisted or just inconvenienced colonial governments were a constant theme under colonial rule. New economic and educational opportunities, better-organized government bureaucracies and expanding political rights were arguably positive features of colonialism, but the colonial regimes remained fundamentally despotic, discriminatory and tainted with violence.

Colonial autocracy was not simply the reflex of military expansionists, it was heartily approved by democratic thinkers. John Stuart Mill, England's leading advocate of political liberties, supported colonial autocracy as a kind of benevolent despotism that would bring backward people to the level of education and enlightenment he saw as preconditions for democratic citizenship. His French friend and admirer, Alexis de Tocqueville, shortly after publishing the second volume of his famous *Democracy in America*, became a vociferous supporter of terrorist tactics in the French conquest and 'pacification' of Algeria. In the 1840s as Deputy in the National Assembly he gave personal backing to General Thomas Bugeaud whose brutal methods in Algeria were receiving criticism at the time. Returning from a visit there in October 1841, de Tocqueville wrote: 'In France I have often heard people I respect, but do not approve, deplore burning harvests, emptying granaries and seizing unarmed men, women and children. As I see it, these are unfortunate necessities that any people wishing to make war on the Arabs must accept... I believe the laws of war entitle us to ravage the country and that we must do this, either by destroying crops at harvest time, or all the time by making rapid incursions, known as raids, the aim of which is to carry off men and flocks.'

When Algerians, led by Abdel Kader, continued to resist French rule and the settlement of Europeans in the colony, de Tocqueville extended his argument: 'Large-scale expeditions seem necessary now and then: first, to continue showing the Arabs and our soldiers that there are no obstacles to our progress through the country; and second, to destroy anything resembling a permanent settlement, or in other words a town. I believe it is of the greatest importance to leave no town standing in the lands of Abdel Kader, now or in the future.'[2] Other European liberals and democrats were, like de Tocqueville, motivated to defend national honor and the military virtues of discipline and loyalty and to give political expression to their belief in the cultural or racial superiority of Europeans. Few were as frank as de Tocqueville in supporting state terrorism in the colonial projects that implemented their beliefs, perhaps because the argument so blatantly contradicts the principle of human equality. Later architects of state terrorism found other ways to justify their actions.

Perfecting state terrorism

The most notorious cases of terrorism by governments against their own citizens are those of Nazi Germany and the Soviet Union under Joseph Stalin. Recent research places Mao's China, especially during the Cultural Revolution, in the same category. Under these regimes special police pursued groups deemed unreliable or unwanted with unprecedented efficiency and ruthlessness. They made political conformity a central ideological tenet to be accomplished by any means necessary, including terror. They targeted particular categories of their citizens for physical elimination and made terrorism a core method for enforcing control over the minds and actions of their subjects. They were successful for many years in keeping citizens frightened and off-balance, and eliminating individuals and groups that might have organized an opposition.

One local study gives a striking portrait of how Nazi terror worked. In the town of Thalburg the Nazi party seized local power in a series of steps over a period of about six months after Hitler was named Chancellor of Germany. Under Nazi control, the police, with the support of locally organized gangs of Brownshirts, used unpredictable arrests, house searches and intimidation to spread fear and uncertainty among the population. Once the local Nazi party gained control of the local government, its leadership could remove all opposition party members from government jobs and roles. Nazi party loyalists took control of every sports club and civic association in the town, not all at once, but one at a time.

According to a theory popular today such associations play a vital role supporting democratic beliefs and practices.[3] On that view the numerous associations in Thalburg should have been centers of resistance to the Nazi takeover. That they were not attests to the efficacy of well-orchestrated state terror. There was no point at which organized opponents could gather their strength and say 'now we must resist'. Instead they were isolated and left not only disorganized but also fearful. Potential organizers were neutralized, sent to concentration camps or driven into exile.

The Nazis took control of all the newspapers and shaped the news coverage to their liking. They turned the schools to the teaching of national socialist doctrines, including antisemitism. Ceremony, ritual and the media outlets kept up a drumbeat of support for Hitler, the local Nazis and Nazi doctrine. After several months the system of terror became routinized and the open use of brutal violence was no longer necessary. On the larger canvas ugly and open violence did not cease; terrorism, war and exterminism marked the evolution of the Third Reich.

The Soviet Union under Stalin systematized the use of terror even before Hitler did in Germany. Stalin met the widespread resistance to collectivization of agriculture in the early 1930s with arrests, torture and forced labor. The network of forced labor camps received another wave of prisoners in the late 1930s as officials forced the pace of collectivization. The great purges of the leadership of the Communist Party and the military officer corps visited terrorism upon holders of power and influence who might have stood in the way of Stalin and his policies of centralization and crash industrialization. The famous show trials with the dramatic confessions of former heroes were only the most publicized part of a system of terror that targeted political and industrial managers, artists, intellectuals and academics who could be removed from their jobs, sent to prison camps or simply killed. Estimates vary widely, but it seems that at least 10 million citizens were sent to forced labor camps in the 1930s and 1940s. Prisoners were forced to live and to work under atrocious conditions. After Stalin's death in 1953 the population of the forced labor camps declined and most were disbanded in 1956. Over the whole course of the camps' existence millions died in the camps, many of them executed. The terror was calculated to keep all possible critics off-balance, fearful, isolated and helpless. As in the town of Thalburg in Hitler's Germany the active use of terror in the USSR gradually declined and became an institutionalized feature of the dictatorship.

State terror during China's Cultural Revolution had original features, some of them reminiscent of the Reign of Terror in France in 1793-94, although in China the violence continued for a decade and killed millions. Starting in 1966, it activated local groups, especially young students, to organize into Red Guards and attack 'capitalist roaders' and 'bourgeois revisionism' and to transform or destroy state institutions from schools and universities to the Chinese Communist Party that the group around Mao sought to weaken or change. It revealed that even an autocratic government promoting a cult of personality can find it difficult to direct the course of violence it instigates and promotes.[4]

The national security state

In the 1970s several Latin American countries adopted a model of government that came to be called the national security state. The military rulers focused all the powers of the state against the forces of 'communism' and social reformism which they believed were destabilizing influences that threatened the geopolitical integrity of the nation. Their key instruments were police and military forces which, together with semi-autonomous rightwing death squads, used terror against the population at large and groups they regarded as politically suspect. After the military coup against Salvador Allende in 1973 in Chile that brought General Augusto Pinochet to power, the Government rounded up a wide spectrum of possible opponents and killed over 3,000 people. In Argentina the campaign of mothers to find out what happened to their sons and daughters, among the 13,000 to 15,000 people who were 'disappeared' under the military government that ruled from 1976 to 1983, has continued for three decades.

US support was instrumental in fostering the rise to power of the national security regimes in Latin America. From Brazil in 1964 to Central America in the 1980s the US gave more than general diplomatic support; it contributed to the nuts and bolts of the security agenda by training soldiers and police. Some

60,000 Latin American soldiers attended courses at the most prominent of several training facilities, the School of the Americas (in Panama from 1946 to 1984 and at Fort Benning, Georgia since then). Training manuals used in courses covered methods of political control and interrogation that included assassination and torture.[5]

The School gained notoriety when a US Congressional investigation of the 1989 murder in El Salvador of six priests, their housekeeper and her daughters discovered that 19 of the 26 soldiers held responsible for the killings had been trained at the School. Under pressure from protests the US Government declassified key documents that:

> brought to light a roll call of senior alumni which read like a who's who of the most brutal military dictators and human-rights violators in Latin America over the past five decades: Manuel Noriega and Omar Torrijos of Panama; Anastasio Somoza of Nicaragua; Leopoldo Galtieri of Argentina; Generals Hector Gramajo and Manuel Antonio Callejas of Guatemala; Hugo Banzar Suarez of Bolivia; the El Salvador death-squad leader Roberto D'Aubuisson. A more detailed examination of the declassified lists reveals that more than 500 soldiers who had received training at the academy have since been held responsible for some of the most hideous atrocities carried out in countries in the region during the years they were racked by civil wars and since.[6]

In response to congressional criticism and efforts to close the School, its name was changed in 2001 to the Western Hemisphere Institute for Security Co-operation (WHISC). School of the Americas Watch, a protest organization that favors closing the institution, holds an annual demonstration near the School each November commemorating the anniversary of the murders in El Salvador in 1989. Venezuela, Costa Rica, Argentina, Uruguay and Bolivia no longer send students to the School. Its defenders point out that instruction in democracy and human rights is now mandatory.

Arsenals of repression

The communist, Nazi and national security states that have adopted terrorism against their own citizens as a routine instrument of rule put forward elaborate ideological justifications for their use of violence and fear. Terrorism was not an unconscious reflex. The ideology generally claimed that evil, deceitful and violent enemies of the Volk, the party or the state were secretly working to undermine and destroy what the government was dedicated to defending. Whether the enemies were Jews, capitalist-roaders, communists, kulaks, subversives or urban guerrillas they deserved to be treated with contempt, coercion and liquidation.

Each ideology had its own specific mix of terrorist measures. Invasive and unpredictable searches, arbitrary arrests, torture, imprisonment in special camps, threats to family and deprivation of employment – all seem to be common elements in the arsenal of state terrorist methods. Other methods were more specific to particular ideologies: extermination of Jews, Roma and homosexuals in purpose-designed death camps with gas chambers were a Nazi invention; show trials, land seizures and deliberate starvation were specialties of Stalinism; death squads, torture cells and dropping victims from aircraft into the sea were prominent features of the national security states of Latin America; ceremonial public humiliation, ridicule, and brutalization held a central place in China's cultural revolution.

Several governments in recent years have used terrorist action against particular ethnic groups. The military government of Myanmar (Burma) has since 1962 used violence against ethnic minorities, particularly the Shan, Karen, Karenni and Rohingya groups. In his report for the year 2000, UN special investigator Rajsoomer Lallah cited summary executions as well as 'extortion, rape, torture, forced labor and portering' (forced carrying of heavy loads). He reported that women were often the victims of these violations. This ongoing use of state terrorism made headlines again in September and October 2007 when large demonstrations by monks, students and others gave hope for political change, but a crackdown followed. The brutal police-state pattern has continued for decades alongside the repression of the National League for Democracy led by Aung San Suu Kyi – the party never allowed to take office after it won the 1990 elections.[7] Under President Suharto, Indonesia's murderous 25-year repression in East Timor killed an estimated 200,000 people, one quarter of the population. The terror was reignited after the East Timorese voted for independence in August 1999 and thousands more were killed in well-planned massacres.

The most notorious recent cases of state terrorism aimed at exterminating a section of a country's population are those of Cambodia and Rwanda. The Cambodian Communist Party or Khmer Rouge, a revolutionary movement led by Pol Pot, gained power in Cambodia after the terrible destruction and disorganization brought about by the US campaign in Cambodia from 1969 to 1973 with its intensive, secret and illegal bombing. Between 1975 and 1978 the Pol Pot regime turned all its efforts to constructing a purified Khmer rural society. It forced the urban population to move to the countryside and executed at least 200,000 people, many of them deemed to be contaminated with imperialism or Vietnamese blood or culture. Intellectuals, professionals, civil servants and cultural leaders were systematically eliminated.

Forced labor on construction and agricultural schemes, starvation and disease killed another 1.5 million Cambodians. About one Cambodian in five was exterminated. The Government's ruthless hold on power continued until it was driven from office by the Vietnamese invasion of 1979.[8]

The genocidal state terrorism in Rwanda in 1994 aimed to fulfill a simple political program: to kill as many of the Tutsi minority as it could and to reconfigure the country according to mythical ideas of an ancient and pure Hutu society. The Hutu-dominated government was faced with a growing guerrilla opposition led by the Rwanda Patriotic Front (RPF), whose core leadership came from the Tutsis who had become refugees in Uganda. In 1993 Hutu leaders around President Juvénal Habyarimana, including some intellectuals and military officers, began to plan for the systematic killing of Tutsis. One important instrument was to be a youth militia, the *Interahamwe*, which already existed and had begun to attack Tutsis. Another scheme was to form a 'civilian defense force' separate from government that could act rapidly when the signal to start killing came.

The opportunity to unleash the plan arrived on 6 April 1994 when persons still unknown shot down the plane in which President Habyarimana was returning from peace negotiations. The group around the President who had planned the extermination decided to act. The first step was to kill government and opposition leaders, mainly Hutu, who were not part of the plan in order to create a power vacuum. Colonel Bagosora and his Presidential Guard took the lead in this operation. He became the leader of the interim government that directed the rapidly expanding waves of killing. The guns and grenades of the militia and the army were crucial, but the leaders found the killing could be speeded up by enlisting popular groups using machetes and other hand-powered weapons. Gangs moving house to house were less effective than forcing or tricking targeted people to gather in a church or school where they could be burned, shot or slashed to death. Radio was used to orchestrate the process and participation was encouraged with promises of access to the land and houses of the victims and by threats of punishment. There are well-documented reports that those leading the operations gave orders to the killers to degrade, mutilate and rape the women they were about to murder.

Over time the genocide planners were able to enlist much of the state apparatus in the killing. Resisters were eliminated. As remarkable as the collaboration of military officers and professional administrators was the absence of any effective international action to halt the killings. In 13 weeks about 500,000 people, three-quarters of the Tutsi population, were killed. Over time the genocide ceased to give the interim government internal cohesion or win popular support. International disapproval finally began to hurt it, but it was the military success of the RPF that brought the regime and its program of genocide to an end.[9]

Episodes of state terrorism

Many governments have made less wholehearted use of terrorism. The organizational chart of most existing governments hides some agency with a terrorism brief and the state's history conceals some episode in which state terrorism became a prominent feature of politics. In France, long before the revolutionary state's Great Terror in which successive leaders of the revolution sent one another to the guillotine, the Roman Catholic establishment waged a campaign in the 11th century against the Cathars in southwestern France who stood against the Roman church and the corruption of the clergy. Northern French nobility backed the church in a crusade against the resisting heretics. The Treaty of Paris confirmed the subordination of the southern nobility that had harbored the Cathars, but it failed to root out the movement, despite the massacre of many of its followers. It took the systematic terrorism of the Inquisition in the 13th and 14th centuries with its reliance on informants, searches of homes, harsh questioning and torture to extinguish the heresy.

In the United States the defeated plantocracy after the civil war used terror to re-establish its dominance and to disempower former slaves. Under the slave system the private property privileges of slave owners had kept the essential violence of the slave system largely in the private realm. After the civil war former slave owners founded the Ku Klux Klan (KKK) to resist the changes in the social hierarchy pursued in Reconstruction. In North Carolina, Tennessee and Georgia, the KKK played a large part in restoring the political dominance of the white elite. The white elite kept the newly enfranchised African-American ex-slaves from entering the public sphere of politics through a combination of terrorism and restrictive legislation. The Ku Klux Klan was their terrorist instrument. Its secret meetings, rituals and cross burnings were designed to frighten, but it was murder, violence and direct intimidation that made it effective. It attacked freed slaves and their white supporters with beatings, arson, lynchings and assassinations. The governments of the southern states benefited from the terrorist acts carried out by the KKK. The intimidation backed up the Jim Crow legislation (segregation in public places, poll taxes, literacy tests for voting) that disenfranchised and disempowered African-Americans.

States often use Klan-like proxy organizations to carry out terrorism against the state's own citizens. The apartheid government in South Africa, for example, in one of many state terrorist operations ordered 'hit squads' associated with Chief Buthelezi's Inkhata party to attack members of the African National Congress.[10] Frequently parts of the government do not support such

State terrorism

actions and may not know about them. In the US the federal government focused enough opposition to the terrorism of the KKK to legislate restrictions that reduced its effectiveness. Behind the exclusionary ideology and the attraction to terrorist violence expressed in episodes of state terrorism lies a profound cynicism about popular politics.

Hitler put it most concisely: 'Cruelty impresses. Cruelty and raw force. The simple man in the street is impressed only by brute force and ruthlessness. Terror is the most effective political means.' It is a political means that poisons the normal politics of debate, negotiation and confrontation.

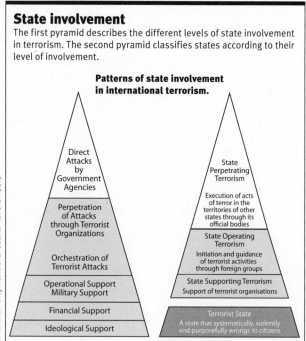

State involvement

The first pyramid describes the different levels of state involvement in terrorism. The second pyramid classifies states according to their level of involvement.

Patterns of state involvement in international terrorism.

Direct Attacks by Government Agencies

Perpetration of Attacks through Terrorist Organizations

Orchestration of Terrorist Attacks

Operational Support Military Support

Financial Support

Ideological Support

State Perpetrating Terrorism

Execution of acts of terror in the territories of other states through its official bodies

State Operating Terrorism

Initiation and guidance of terrorist activities through foreign groups

State Supporting Terrorism

Support of terrorist organisations

Terrorist State

A state that systematically, violently and purposefully wrongs its citizens

www.milnet.com; *Countering State-Sponsored Terrorism*, Boaz Ganor, The International Policy Institute for Counter-Terrorism (ICT).

Transnational state terrorism

Another variety of state terrorism is government-sponsored acts of violence across borders to harm, kill and intimidate civilians of another country. The term 'terrorist state' as it is used in the press and by governments usually refers to this kind of terrorism. Although governments bent on troubling other states or movements in other countries sometimes act through official government agencies, they usually prefer to act through proxy organizations, sometimes called 'cutouts,' and to keep their own role invisible.

The aim of transnational state terrorism may be to destabilize and weaken a government that is perceived to be hostile and perhaps a supporter of groups regarded as terrorist opponents. The accusations, and at times the reality, of terrorism are flung in both directions. Apartheid South Africa went to great lengths to counter the popular movements for decolonization in Southern Africa. As Angola and Mozambique moved toward independence, apartheid South Africa made extensive use of terror (as well as outright warfare) to keep the newly independent governments weak and disorganized. Their 'total strategy' of defense was similar to the pattern of the national security states of South America. In 1976 their armed forces took over support for Renamo (*Resistencia Nacional Mocambicana*), the terrorist opposition to the new government in Mozambique formed by Frelimo (Front for the Liberation of Mozambique). Renamo had been nurtured by the Rhodesian security forces, who had recruited dissident Frelimo fighters to destabilize the new Frelimo Government. Renamo became infamous for the brutality of its attacks on civilians and for its targeting of schools and health clinics as well as economic installations like roads, electric lines and pipelines.

A pattern of reciprocal violence that includes terrorism sometimes repeats itself in the relations between hostile neighboring countries. Each government supports terrorist or guerrilla operations inside its rival. India and Pakistan repeatedly accuse each other of terrorism in the disputed territory of Kashmir. Sudan long supported the terrorist Lord's Resistance Army in Uganda while Uganda gave sustenance to the Sudan People's Liberation Movement, which fought a guerrilla war for the right for self-determination of southern Sudan. The 2005 peace agreement in southern Sudan and a ceasefire and negotiations in Uganda in 2007 may keep this pattern of reciprocal violence from re-igniting.

In the Middle East, support for Palestinian groups that engage in terrorism in Israel has come from Saudi Arabia, Syria, Iraq and Iran. The government of Israel has often blamed the Palestinian Authority, a quasi-state, for many of the suicide bombings of civilian gatherings in Israel claimed by Hamas, Islamic Jihad, Tanzim and the Al-Aqsa Martyrs Brigade. On its side the government of Israel has sent its defense forces to assassinate people it says are responsible for terrorism and it has militarized its occupation of Palestinian settlements and refugee camps in the West Bank. In these operations its forces have killed many civilians.[11] Both sides claim to be fighting for the just cause of national survival against a violent enemy. This does not make their attacks against civilians any less terrorist, but it does make it difficult for each side to change tracks from violence to diplomacy in pursuit of their cause.

The Cold War and containment

The Cold War generated widely spread reciprocal support for rival terrorisms from the United States and the Soviet Union. The two superpowers were drawn to almost every conflict in the world if only to ensure that the other side did not gain some advantage from it. In all the conflicts mentioned above one can find US and Soviet fingerprints somewhere along the way. The superpowers gave important direct and indirect support to organizations that made extensive use of terrorism, including training them in terrorist techniques. The scale of superpower involvement in terrorism gives the lie to the common view that terrorism is exclusively 'the weapon of the weak.' Often it is the weapon with which the strong get the weak to do their dirty work for them.

In its preoccupation with containing communism, the US saw danger in the decolonizing world and in many other places besides. President John Kennedy's Government initiated a long-running effort to bring down the Castro regime. After the failed Bay of Pigs invasion in 1961, US-trained anti-Castro Cubans repeatedly committed acts of violence against Cuba. As recently as the mid 1990s they planted bombs designed to cripple the growing Cuban tourist industry.[12] (The same groups have been convicted of attacks in Miami against Cubans doing business with Cuba.[13])

In the 1980s the Reagan Administration sounded the alarm about a 'terror network' orchestrated by the Soviet Union threatening US and Western interests around the globe and especially in Southern Africa, Central America, the Middle East and Central Asia. Fear of instability and distrust of nationalist regimes and movements drew the US to embrace governments that abused human rights, to support agencies that engaged in terrorism and to sponsor certain terrorist activities of its own. In Angola, Nicaragua, Afghanistan and Kampuchea (Cambodia) the US supported, and sometimes created, insurgencies that they tried to present as democratic and freedom-seeking. Often these groups practiced terrorism.

The Soviet Union was not squeamish about supporting violence, but most anti-colonial movements were largely peaceful and those that engaged in violence, even those professing Marxism and receiving

Soviet support, gravitated to guerrilla warfare and directed their arms at military and police targets. Some, like the African National Congress in South Africa, committed occasional acts of terrorism. In settler-colonies like Kenya, Algeria and Angola, movements did turn to terrorism against settlers and against those Africans who collaborated with

Algeria

Late in Gillo Pontecorvo's popular, neo-realist film, *The Battle of Algiers* (1967), which unflinchingly chronicles the guerilla war, a scene occurs in which Ben H'midi, the captured political leader of the FLN, is asked by a French journalist how he could justify murdering innocent French civilians. In a reference to the French use of napalm and carpet-bombing in the countryside, H'midi replies: 'Let us have your bombers and you can have our women's baskets.' In other words, atrocities are atrocities. And if the oppressed appear to use more 'primitive' means, it is because they are forced onto unequal ground.

In quoting H'midi, I do not wish to justify the Palestinian bombers. In both cases, the Algerian and Palestinian, we should lament the fact that in neither case was a Gandhian form of resistance able to take hold...

France's campaign in Algiers instantly became a classic of counter-insurgency warfare. To break the FLN's network, French paratroopers cordoned off the Casbah and rounded up thousands of Algerian men (without charge). The French tortured and executed (without trial) thousands of young Algerian men and women. Eventually, such ruthless tactics worked. The French smashed the network of urban guerilla cells...

Algeria achieved its independence in 1962... The human toll, meanwhile, still shocks the conscience. Twenty thousand French died uselessly to preserve the colony. One million Algerians died for their freedom.

The legacy of this violence continues to haunt both cultures. In Algeria, violence became the de facto political weapon of choice in the brutal civil war of the 1980s and 1990s. France, meanwhile, still struggles to come to terms with its colonial crimes, as indicated in the recent trial of the (unrepentant) French General responsible for torturing and killing Algerians.

John Sanbonmatsu, 'Will the Battle for Jerusalem Become the Battle of Algiers? Suicide Bombings and Colonialism – Then and Now', April 2002, http://opgreens.org

or worked for them. Those actions were usually not linked to Soviet support.

The Soviets did support governments that engaged in state terrorism including those of Muammar al-Qaddafi in Libya and Mengistu Haile Mariam in Ethiopia. Other communist governments, including those in Cuba, Cambodia, North Vietnam, Eastern Europe and China made use of terrorism in consolidating and retaining political control. No doubt the example of Stalinism played a part in choosing purges, assassinations and imprisonment over negotiation and accommodation.

Overthrow

In 1953 and 1954 the US Government through the CIA engineered the overthrow of nationalist and reformist governments in Iran and Guatemala and the installation of regimes that used terrorism to weaken and control political opposition and drive local communist parties underground. In preparation for these operations of 'regime change' the CIA gathered detailed intelligence about potential friends and foes, disseminated propaganda in the form of leaflets, manipulated news reports to encourage opposition and concocted evidence of Soviet involvement. The agency also identified alternative rulers and induced them to take action, promising financial and diplomatic backing to a new government.[14] In 1953 the CIA with Britain's Secret Intelligence Service (SIS) spearheaded the coup against Prime Minister Mohammad Mosaddeq of Iran to counter his nationalization of the British Petroleum Company and to move against the communist Tudeh party whose influence they feared was growing. They induced the Shah to abandon his original indifference to politics and to support the change in government. To foment street demonstrations, CIA agents posing as communists threatened Muslim clerics with 'savage punishment if they opposed Mosaddeq' and bombed the home of a prominent Muslim. These were two measures of direct terrorism committed by US agencies.[15] In 1954 the US followed a similar plan in Guatemala. After an intense public relations campaign financed by the United Fruit Company (in which Secretary of State John Foster Dulles and CIA Director Allen Dulles had personal financial interest) President Eisenhower approved another project of regime change. The CIA took the lead in organizing a dissident army to invade from neighboring Honduras to overthrow the government of Jacabo Arbenz whose policies of land reform, higher corporate taxes and university education for lower-class youth troubled the United Fruit Company and the established elite and sparked worry that the influence of communism would grow. The US provided air cover and the CIA mounted a large disinformation campaign exaggerating the size and effectiveness of the invasion. There was some US-sponsored violence in Guatemala: boarding peaceful vessels off the coast and bombing a few targets inside the country.[16]

In both these cases the real link to terror came when the replacement regimes arrested, tortured and killed opponents and dissidents. The CIA helped train the security forces of the new governments and maintained close ongoing relations with them. Iran's State Intelligence and Security Organization (SAVAK) was established in 1957 with the guidance of US and Israeli intelligence services. It first sought to arrest members of the Tudeh party, but it grew into a full-scale secret police operation with high tech equipment from the US to monitor and collate information on all aspects of political and civic activity. It kept newspapers, journalists, labor unions, peasants' organizations and other civic associations under tight surveillance. It established its own prisons and made extensive use of brutal methods of torture. Observers estimate that in response to the demonstrations of

1978, SAVAK killed 13,000 to 15,000 Iranian citizens and seriously injured another 50,000.[17] It became famous for hunting down regime opponents around the world. Throughout its existence the CIA remained its close collaborator.

A detailed CIA study of the Iran coup draws as one lesson that the CIA's military planners should have political arrest lists ready.[18] In Guatemala they certainly had such a list for what the CIA planning document called 'the roll-up of Communists and collaborators.' After the coup the police rounded up and killed hundreds of people. A system of deadly repression making extensive use of death squads dressed as civilians, but taking orders from security forces, was put in place. The resistance, weak as it was, of indigenous peoples and the obligation to fight communism were the repeated excuses for a reign of terror that killed some 100,000 Guatemalans over the next four decades. The US remained a close and supportive partner of the government of Guatemala through most of these years, giving assistance in designing and setting up an urban counter-terrorist task force and in supplying military advisers and equipment. At times the US representatives in Guatemala City thought the counter-insurgency was running out of control, but on balance they defended it. They rained criticism on the human rights organizations that catalogued and publicized government terrorist atrocities, labeling them misguided or communist sympathizers.[19]

The record shows that government terror and killing of Mayan villagers in Guatemala peaked in the early 1980s just when the US was pumping up its overt and clandestine campaign to overthrow the Nicaraguan Government of the Frente Sandinista de Liberación National (FSLN or Sandinistas) that had gained power in 1979 when the US-supported military apparatus of dictator Anastasio Somoza collapsed. President Ronald Reagan's Government was fearful of what they considered to be expanding communist influence in Central America and the Caribbean and especially vexed by the successful guerrilla war of the leftwing Sandinista movement. Policy planners centered in the National Security Agency and the CIA put into practice the doctrine of 'low intensity warfare' to force the replacement of the Sandinistas by a conservative and pliant set of rulers.

At the heart of the method was the creation of a guerrilla army out of members of Somoza's National Guard and several other splinter groups revolving around Eden Pastora, a dissident former Sandinista. Documents recently released under the Freedom of Information Act show that the Contras, as the grouping was known, were wholly created and controlled by the US. Much of the work on the ground of finding and paying leaders, writing policy statements and providing operational manuals was handled by Oliver North, later well known as a key figure in the Iran-Contra scandal. By creating and supporting the Contras the US engaged in terrorism by proxy. The Contras were instructed to hit 'soft targets' like agricultural co-operatives and some of them were advised by US experts and manuals about 'how to use selective violence' and 'coercive counterintelligence interrogation of resistant sources.' The Contras often attacked civilians, even rounded them up and shot them.

In order to make the Contras look more effective than they were and to cripple the economy of Nicaragua the US conducted direct military operations, attacking economic targets like oil depots and allowing the Contras to take the credit. To back up the impression that the Contras were an indigenous reality the US mounted a sophisticated public relations and news-generating effort. Contra leaders were escorted around the US on speaking tours. Corrupt exiled Nicaraguan leaders sometimes associated with the drug trade were obliged to meet, declare unity and sign a policy statement written under the guidance of Oliver North. The specific aim was to represent the Contras as legitimate fighters for the liberation of their country from a communist elite. A public relations firm was hired to get the news out and President Reagan uttered his famous comparison: the Contras are 'the moral equivalent of our founding fathers.' The Atlantic and Caribbean ports of Nicaragua were mined by the US

Torture was taught by the CIA

Washington – A newly declassified CIA training manual details torture methods used against suspected subversives in Central America during the 1980s, refuting claims by the agency that no such methods were taught there.

'Human Resource Exploitation Training Manual – 1983' was released Friday in response to a Freedom of Information Act (FOIA) request filed by *The Baltimore Sun* on 26 May 1994.

The CIA also declassified a Vietnam-era training manual called 'KUBARK Counterintelligence Interrogation – July 1963', which also taught torture and is believed by intelligence sources to have been a basis for the 1983 manual.

Torture methods taught in the 1983 manual include stripping suspects naked and keeping them blindfolded. Interrogation rooms should be windowless, dark and soundproof, with no toilet.

'The "questioning" room is the battlefield upon which the "questioner" and the subject meet,' the 1983 manual states. 'However, the "questioner" has the advantage in that he has total control over the subject and his environment.'

The 1983 manual was altered between 1984 and early 1985 to discourage torture after a furor was raised in Congress and the press about CIA training techniques being used in Central America. Those alterations and new instructions appear in the documents obtained by *The Baltimore Sun*, and support the conclusion that methods taught in the earlier version were illegal.

Human rights abuses by the Honduran unit known as Battalion 316 were most intense in the early 1980s at the height of the Reagan Administration's war against communism in Central America...

The methods taught in the 1983 manual and those used by Battalion 316 in the early 1980s show unmistakable similarities.

Gary Cohn, Ginger Thompson, and Mark Matthews, *The Baltimore Sun*, 27 January 1997.

with the goal of raising the costs of marine insurance high enough to strangle Nicaragua's vital seaborne trade. And US troops staged military maneuvers on Nicaragua's borders in order to force an expensive and distracting military response from the Sandinista Government.

The US has had a role in overthrowing several other governments on the grounds of their unreliability in the Cold War alignment. The assassination of Patrice Lumumba in the Congo in 1961 and the installation of Joseph Mobutu as President inaugurated a cycle of corrupt and tyrannical government. The change from Sukarno to Suharto in Indonesia in 1965 precipitated mass killings of 500,000 to one million people. To clear the way for the coup d'état against Salvador Allende's Government in Chile in 1973 the CIA worked actively with members of the Chilean military to 'neutralize' General Rene Schneider, Commander-in-Chief of the Chilean Army. Schneider was a strong constitutionalist known to oppose a coup against the legally elected President. When a group of officers with whom the CIA had been collaborating killed General Schneider in 1970, the US assisted in protecting the assassins.[20] It was the first political assassination in Chile since 1837.

Changes of government are usually complex events and the interventions are clandestine and may come from more than one country. The interveners try to make use of local social and military forces that have a life of their own. The terrorist element in the US role in these coups d'état seems often to have been that of an accomplice – supplying encouragement, money and weapons, assurance of future support and a list of dangerous individuals and organizations. More telling is the continued involvement of the US military and security specialists, assisting the design and organization of a security apparatus and the training of people in the skills of interrogation and 'counter-insurgency' operations. US officials know full well that such an apparatus and the skills learned are often turned to the systematic and long-term employment of terror to keep a government in power.

Blowback and instability

From the standpoint of the US strategists there are two big dangers: blowback and instability. Blowback is the CIA term for the unintended, unforeseen and unwanted consequences of secret operations. It is used frequently to describe the actions of organizations that the US created and strengthened that later turn against US-related targets. One kind of blowback is terrorism against US interests. The US invested money, training and equipment to make the Taliban and other fundamentalist groups in Pakistan and Afghanistan effective fighters against Soviet domination of Afghanistan. The Soviets were driven out and the Soviet regime was weakened. Regime change in favor of the Taliban brought stability to a chronically unstable land. But when men trained at the training camps for the Afghan jihad planted bombs in Saudi Arabia and Egypt, critics saw blowback. In targeting governments allied with the US the fighters formerly serving Western interests in the Cold War re-emerged as anti-Western terrorists. With Taliban support for al-Qaeda the blowback continued.

The possibility of instability can also promote terrorism. The strategy of inducing regime change by intervening covertly to support a coup usually assumes that a freshly-formed military government willing to use well-structured security methods can control political forces and stay in power. Factional fights, inexperience and regional tensions make stability a rare commodity. The support for Lon Nol's coup against the mercurial Prince Sihanouk in Cambodia in 1970 is a good example – a search for stability contributing to repression and backlash. The US interest in stability pushes it to give increasing support to those who control the repressive apparatus in the new government and to condone, if not deliberately enhance, its reliance on state terror. In the name of Cold War goals the US often found itself aiding and abetting unstable regimes heavily engaged in state terrorism.

State terrorism after the Cold War

Since the end of the Cold War many dictatorships have been replaced by elected governments (southern cone of South America, Central America, South Africa, Indonesia). The reasons for these changes include the strength and skill of popular movements and the reduction of US support for repressive governments. Similarly the break-up of the Soviet Union and the end of Soviet control over Eastern Europe removed a pattern of Soviet-supported state terrorism in some twenty countries from East Germany to Kyrgyzstan.

Yet state terrorism remains a reality and a potential. The genocide in Rwanda, the violence of Robert Mugabe's Government in Zimbabwe against the legal opposition, the actions of Russia in Chechnya, the use of violence by the government of Uzbekistan, and the continuing dictatorship in North Korea show that state terrorism has causes beyond the Cold War. The US may be less prone to support terrorist states than in the days of the Cold War, but the response to attacks in New York and Washington raise the possibility that in the war on terrorism under the banner of 'those not with us are against us' the US may support 'friendly' governments that engage in state terrorist campaigns. Russia (Chechnya), Pakistan (Kashmir), Uzbekistan, Tajikistan and Kyrgyzstan all seem to fit this pattern.[21,22]

The possibility that the US is still willing to give support to governments and groups that make extensive use of terrorism raises a deeper question. Could the new global manicheanism of good democrats versus evil terrorists be a conscious effort to reconstruct a doctrinal defense of support for governments and policies that favor the corporate global economic agenda even if they repress genuinely popular movements? The War on Terror is given by several governments as reason for abandoning the prohibition against torture, increasing surveillance, expanding the use of secretly deployed special forces and lending support to repressive governments that are seen as allies against terrorism. Russia uses a similar logic and supports governments within its historic sphere of influence that engage in terrorism.

The amount of state terrorist activity and its continuing appeal is not surprising given the huge concentration of control over weapons that governments enjoy. Furthermore, governments have a huge stake in protecting their political power from rivals and enemies. It is little wonder that government leaders can be tempted to use terrorism to translate the money, arms and intelligence at their disposal into enhancement of their grip on power and their capacity to pursue other political aims. Perhaps the surprising thing is that governments are not more prone to terrorism than they are. The frequency of deleterious 'blowback' may deter some leaders. Certainly political action in defense of civil liberties and in favor of full disclosure of government action can help discourage government leaders prone to terrorist temptation and strengthen the hold of a culture of open political encounter.

State terrorism has a life cycle distinct from that of group terrorism. Terrorist states are often brought down in large-scale wars or driven from power by broad political movements or coups d'état that reflect political processes beyond the terrorist dynamic. Where state terrorism is part of a program to counter hostile terrorist groups, it may diminish and end along with the terrorism against which it struggles. Where a terrorist regime is overthrown or defeated in elections, a new government is more likely to abandon repressive policies. It will still face the difficult question of whether to pursue justice against incumbent or former officials who engaged in terrorism.

Digging deeper into ways of understanding terrorism is the job of the next chapter.

1 Elizabeth A Fenn, 'Biological Warfare in Eighteenth-Century North America: Beyond Jeffery Amherst', Journal of American History 86, no 4, March 2000: 1554–58. **2** Olivier Le Cour Grandmaison, 'Liberty, equality and colony,' *Le Monde Diplomatique* 11 July 2001, http://mondediplo.com/2001/06/11torture **3** Robert Putnam, 'Bowling Alone', *Journal of Democracy* 6, no 1, January 1995. **4** Jonathan D Spence, 'China's Great Terror', *The New York Review of Books* 53, no 14, 21 September 2006. **5** Robert Parry, 'Lost History: "Project X" and School of Assassins', The Consortium of Independent Journalism, www.consortiumnews.com/archive **6** Christine Toomey, 'The Killing Fields', *Sunday Times Magazine*, 18 November 2001. **7** Rajsoomer Lallah, Situation of Human Rights in Myanmar, United Nations Economic and Social Council, Commission on Human Rights, 2000, www.unhchr.ch/Huridocda; BBC, Protests in Burma, 2 October 2007, http://news.bbc.co.uk/2/hi/asia-pacific **8** Ben Kiernan, *The Pol Pot Regime: Race, Power, and Genocide in Cambodia Under the Khmer Rouge*, 1975-79, Yale University Press, 1996. **9** Human Rights Watch, *Leave None to Tell the Story: Genocide in Rwanda*, 1999, www.hrw.org/reports/1999/rwanda. **10** Norm Dixon, 'New evidence: apartheid terror ordered from the top', Green Left Weekly, no 344, 9 June, 1996, www.hartford-hwp.com/archives **11** Fares A Braizat, 'What counts as terrorism? The view on the Arab street', OpenDemocracy, 1 January 2005. **12** Saul Landau, 'A Double Standard on Terrorism', *In These Times* magazine, 4 March 2002. **13** US Department of Justice, Federal Bureau of Investigation, 'Cuban Anti-Castro Terrorism', Washington DC 20535, 16 May 1990. **14** William Blum, *The CIA: A Forgotten History*, Zed Books, 1986. **15** www.nytimes.com/library/world/mideast/041600iran-cia-chapter2.html **16** Blum, *The CIA: A Forgotten History*; http://hrdata.aaas.org/ciidh/ **17** www.fas.org/irp/world/iran/savak/ **18** Donald N Wilber, Clandestine Service History: The Overthrow of Premier Mossadeq of Iran November 1952-August 1953, Washington DC: CIA 1969, www.nytimes.com/library, Appendix E: Military Critique – Lessons Learned from TPAJX re Military Planning Aspects of Coup d'Etat. **19** National Security Archive Electronic Briefing Book No 11, US Policy in Guatemala, 1966-1996; Kate Doyle, Project Director; Carlos Osorio, Project Associate. Available at www.gwu.edu. **20** US Government, 'CIA Activities in Chile', 18 September 2000, www.cia.gov/cia/publications **21** Ahmed Rashid, 'They're Only Sleeping', *The New Yorker*, 11 February 2002. **22** Stephen Zunes, 'Bush Administration Support for Repression in Uzbekistan Belies Pro-Democracy Rhetoric', Foreign Policy in Focus, 20 June 2005, Silver City, NM & Washington, DC, www.fpif.org/commentary/2005; Stephen Blank, 'Is There a Basis for Re-Engaging Uzbekistan?' Central Asia-Caucasus Institute Analyst, 23 August 2006, www.cacianalyst.org

4 Morality and history

Ever since President Bush declared a war on terrorism the rhetorical output has continued in clear attempts to shape people's thinking about terrorism and gain their support for action of one kind or another. A map of the moral and historical arguments that opinion-shapers deploy is useful for developing one's own independent viewpoint.

THE LOUDEST AND most public discussion of terrorism has focused on moral conflict. Here both terrorists and counter-terrorists have a lot to say, often describing the situation very starkly as one of Good versus Evil. It is a rhetorical stance that has a short-term political payoff. The speaker gets credit for taking a strong moral position while the listeners can invest the abstract categories with whatever content they choose to bring. The stratagem soon wears thin, however, because it does nothing to extend moral understanding. It simply plugs into existing prejudices and stifles a searching discussion of causes and implications of terrorism.

Moral arguments about terrorism draw on at least three different core ideas: moral community, human rights and the consequences of actions. To add to the confusion, some of the debate is about what grounding is the right one and commentators sometimes shift ground depending on whose actions are being judged, theirs or the enemy's. The different positions are easier to grasp and to evaluate if you know what principles are being invoked.[1]

Moral community. Both the choice to commit terrorism and the feeling of outrage against it stem from a sense of membership in a moral community whose members protect each other. Such a sense of membership is often nourished by stories about the founding of the community, stories in which terrorism and counter-terrorism may figure prominently. The

story of the founding of the US includes both the
Indian Wars of the colonial period and the War of
Independence. In either conflict terrorism was an
adjunct to warfare. Gangs murdered families and
burned settlements. Israel finds its beginnings in the
suffering of the massive terrorism of the Holocaust and
in a few militant terrorist actions. Massacres in several
Palestinian villages spurred the flight of the established
population. A truck bomb at the King David Hotel in
Jerusalem killed dozens of British citizens and pressured
the British to withdraw troops and to leave the Israeli
fighters to secure control territory for their new state.
India and Pakistan were born in a disruptive division
of the British colony that included huge killings of
Hindus in Pakistan and Muslims in India.

If Palestine becomes a state, terrorism will have been
part of its foundation. Other nationalist movements –
Irish, Basque, Corsican, Tamil, Kurdish, Serbian and
others – also have (or had) terrorist offshoots that
believe violence against civilians is justified under the
circumstances – a way their moral community can gain
expression as a state. In Algeria, Angola, Kenya and
elsewhere terrorism contributed to winning political
independence. Frantz Fanon, the insightful critic of
colonialism and false decolonization, thought in 1959
that attacks against settlers could help unite a population
splintered and demoralized by the pervasive violence of
colonial oppression. Fanon believed a violent struggle –
at first desperate and uncoordinated – would gradually
create a common identity among peasants, intellectuals,
workers and urban unemployed. Together they would
begin to construct a healthy political community.[2]

Fanon had a point: and now almost 50 years
later terrorism has joined the experience of war as
a shared bleeding and bloodletting that can define a
national community. But he clearly underestimates
the destructive effect of terrorism. As a psychiatrist in
Algeria in the 1950s who treated both tortured and

torturers Fanon witnessed and recorded an oft-repeated dialectic: colonial oppression provokes anti-colonial terrorism that is met in turn with counter-terrorist terrorism. Who first used terrorism is hotly disputed. Nations, like Algeria, born in a cycle of reciprocal violence have proved no better at establishing workable practices of peaceful political conflict than were those which achieved independence through negotiation. Arguably they are worse.

Rationale

The most common rationale for state terrorism is defense of the moral community that is the nation. In killing Jews, Roma and homosexuals the Nazis asserted they were defending the Aryan nation against racial and moral pollution. Ethnic cleansing in Cambodia, Rwanda, Serbia and elsewhere has been justified along similar lines. Stalin claimed both mother Russia and the international working class as communities whose opponents and betrayers ought to be eliminated.

A sense of moral community also colors the *response* to acts of terrorism. The metaphor of war in defense of a 'good community' is often used to justify extraordinary and arbitrary state powers. US commentators express outrage at the way terrorists abuse democratic freedoms to launch their deadly attacks and portray them as especially vile enemies of civic morality who have lost all claim to the ordinary rights of community members. The US Government has drawn practical conclusions from this moral position. The USA Patriot Act allows the indefinite detention of any resident non-citizens that the Attorney General believes may cause a terrorist act. The underlying rationale is that they are not part of the community of Americans protected by the Constitution. The US Government takes the argument one step further when it claims that under the Congressional Authorization for Use of Military Force, passed one week after the 11 September 2001 attacks,

US citizens believed by federal authorities to have aided those attacks can be labeled 'enemy combatants' and imprisoned until hostilities cease.[3] In effect they lose the rights conferred by community membership. Human rights groups and prisoners have challenged these assertions in court with some success, but key issues are still under adjudication.[4]

Many active political movements today claim that religious belief is the proper basis for a morally-grounded political community. Every religion has the potential of inspiring followers to back their beliefs with political authority. Religions assert grand truths about good and evil and the rules that ought to govern human interactions. The more urgently the claims are felt and the more dangerous the battalions of evil appear to be, the more attractive is the appeal to give their faith a political form. This may include taking armed and deadly action to rout the enemies and preserve the faith. Adherents of political religions that differ profoundly over religious doctrine all agree that the secular political ideal is morally bankrupt. Their descriptions of the materialist, world-dominating enemy can be startlingly similar. Terrorist groups inspired by their versions of Christianity and Islam denounce look-alike conspiracies of Jews, communists, capitalists and Freemasons led by the US Government and the United Nations.

In situations of conflict, commitment to moral community is often the main justification for going to war. Such is the justification of the declaration by George W Bush of the right of the US to strike first at rogue states, terrorist states and terrorists. He believes that striking against enemies of the US moral community is always defensive and always justified. Once a government or a group sees itself as engaged in a war to defend the community it represents, it is a small step to employ weapons that will kill many civilians, torture prisoners to gain essential intelligence or send a suicide bomber on a mission. The *'jihad'*

President George W Bush: against terrorists, strike first

Deterrence, the promise of massive retaliation against nations, means nothing, against shadowy, terrorist networks with no nation or citizens to defend. Containment is not possible when unbalanced dictators with weapons of mass destruction can deliver those weapons on missiles or secretly provide them to terrorists' allies....

The gravest danger to freedom lies at the perilous cross-roads of radicalism and technology. When the spread of chemical and biological and nuclear weapons, along with ballistic missile technology – when that occurs, even weak states and small groups could attain a catastrophic power to strike great nations. Our enemies have declared this very intention, and have been caught seeking these terrible weapons. They want the capability to blackmail us, or to harm us, or to harm our friends – and we will oppose them with all our power....

We must take the battle to the enemy, disrupt his plans and confront the worst threats before they emerge. And our security will require all Americans to be forward-looking and resolute, to be ready for pre-emptive action when necessary to defend our liberty and to defend our lives.

Speech at West Point, 1 June 2002.

proclaimed by Osama bin Laden takes such a step with his call for attacks on US citizens, as well as officials and military personnel. Such proclamations are often merely symbolic rather than practical, but they are still designed to reinforce a sense of moral community among potential followers.

Moral commitment to a group, of course, has real virtues. It can smooth collaboration among community members and make authority legitimate. It may even give grounds for recognizing that other communities have valid claims. To be consistent, nationalists have to admit other nations may also have a moral right to a homeland. Reciprocity is one of the bases for a possible resolution to conflicts. Palestinians and Israelis for example could reciprocally recognize a 'two-state' solution. Both sides have a moral claim to a state complete with a sovereign government and territory in Israel/Palestine. The issue then is where to draw boundaries and how to assure mutual security. However, the attachment of the claims of moral community to particular areas of land complicates the matter. Some Israelis living in West Bank settlements regard their right to this land as absolute and God-given. Palestinians must exercise their national rights elsewhere. Some Palestinian organizations, like Hamas, believe all Israeli claims to land in the region are invalid. Israelis must exercise their national rights elsewhere, not on the stolen land they now occupy. The identification of territory with an identity-based moral community stands in the way of negotiated solutions in many conflicts marked by terrorism around the world.

Religious morality

People who take their political values from Christianity and Islam, religions that claim universal validity, may assert that their rules of morality are valid for all people no matter what they believe. Some fervent believers think that in forcing nonbelievers to comply with the true morality, they are doing God's work. Colonial autocrats forced their subjects to work without pay and expropriated their best land in the name of a Christian civilizing mission – the right of a more evolved community over a more primitive one. The many-layered term 'jihad' in Islamic thinking is best translated as 'struggle.' It can refer to a personal spiritual struggle to accept the full truth of Islam. For some Muslims it can also refer to a defense of Islam by violence if necessary against the aggression of nonbelievers and believers in false forms of Islam. During the crusades and inquisitions Christians, too, have defended a conception of their religious community with arms and resorted to terrorism. To the many people standing outside these circles of religious 'truth', the claims to universal validity seem false and intrusive. The values they assert belong to large, but still limited, moral communities.

This notion of moral community tends to confirm

a non-negotiable starting point and to justify extreme measures: If we = good, then any enemy = evil. Any conflict moves into a stark bipolarism pushing for the exclusion of outsiders and often into warfare. There can be no compromise with evil. If you are not with us, you are against us. There is no difference between leaders and followers, soldiers and civilians, instigators and (possibly reluctant or ignorant) supporters. In such a simplified and distorted world, terrorism against those who stand outside the 'true moral community' is absurdly easy to justify. Immoral actions thus are warranted as means for defending morality itself.

Universal rights. A larger moral framework recognizes that many different and competing claims to a moral community exist. It attaches political authority not to any particular religious or cultural vision, but to the right of anyone to have and to pursue such visions. Moral understanding need not stop at the boundary of one community; it grounds itself in universal values.

A set of influential intellectuals in the United States issued a statement about the evil of the 11 September terrorists and the justice of prosecuting a war against them that put the argument in terms of universal moral principles. The US had to defend such universals as civic freedom, freedom of religion and protection of the human person. War is morally necessary when it is required to defend innocent people whose rights are under attack and who are in no position to defend themselves. A war so justified must be fought by a legitimate authority employing violence proportionate to the danger. The statement made clear that not all the cultural values, social tendencies and government policies in the US are worthy of support. But it argued that the core US values are valid and universal. A war fought to defend these values against terrorists is a just war. Such a war must never target non-combatants, although unintended killing of innocents may be unavoidable.

Morality and history

In the abstract the argument appears strong: a secular state committed to human rights may have to defend the right to have such rights and may have to do so in another country. The signers agree, it seems, with President Bush's words on 1 June 2002 to cadets at West Point: 'America has no empire to extend or utopia to build. We wish for others only what we wish for ourselves – safety from violence, the rewards of liberty, and the hope for a better life.' And, more than that, it can use its military might and other assistance to put its good faith to practical use. In practice the argument comes down to a political judgment. As the editor of the *Wall Street Journal*, Robert Hartley, put it in the 17 June 2002 edition, the supporters are saying that the US, whatever its faults, is 'a force for good in the world'. Supporters of the wars against terrorism in Afghanistan and Iraq who later admitted that they got it wrong often argue that the fault was not in resorting to warfare; it was fighting the war incompetently.[5] Writing in 2007 Michael Ignatieff explains that his mistake on Iraq was to let his anger at Saddam Hussein's state terrorism against Iraq's Kurds blind him to the deep obstacles to unity in Iraq and to the flaws in President Bush's understanding of Iraq and of himself.[6]

Pre-emptive strike

Bush lost the support of some of the signers for another claim announced in the same speech: his government reserved the right to strike first at any government or group that the US believes is about to launch an attack on the US or its allies. Here we see how crucial is the question of who defines and enforces universal human rights. The US has been most reluctant to recognize the authority of any international body to do so. Statement signatories who supported the US war against terrorists and the government of Afghanistan but who do not agree that first strikes are a proportionate military response face a dilemma:

does the US remain a force for good? Does it defend valid universal moral principles? And if it does, is it not guilty of hypocrisy by not applying those same standards to its own actions?

The very universal rights championed by the US are also the starting point for some of the critics of the war on terrorism, many of them US citizens. These critics accept the same constitutional and moral precepts that support democratic governance and civil and human rights but arrive at different political judgments. They believe that on balance the US is not a force for good in the world. Critics like Noam Chomsky readily marshal the evidence – the overthrow of elected governments in Iran, Guatemala, Indonesia and Chile; the training and financing of the Contra terrorists in Nicaragua; the support for President Suharto of Indonesia in his genocidal take-over of Timor Leste (East Timor); the material assistance to President Saddam Hussein in Iraq when he was suppressing Kurdish nationalists with poison gas; and the co-operation with Pakistan and Saudi Arabia in training and arming the Taliban to destabilize the government of Afghanistan. Chomsky believes the world's most powerful government uses violence quite routinely and quite effectively to defend its economic interests. In doing so it stands against the 'hope for a better life' of most of the world's people. This position concludes that the most important step that the US can take to decrease terrorism is to stop engaging in it.

The invective in the altercations between these two 'universal rights' positions is especially acrimonious. They agree on the moral premise that humans universally have a right to freedom, security and democracy. They even agree that the record of the US in supporting these rights is not pure. They further agree that the people who brought down the World Trade Center and damaged the Pentagon are a real menace and must be stopped. The two groups disagree about whether the US Government should be the sole arbiter of who is and who is not a threat to universal human rights. The critics of the US want to strengthen international courts and bodies to make such judgments and enforce them. The supporters of the US record trust the US to make the correct determination over the long run.

Consequentialism. Many who think about the moral meaning of terrorism are less interested in the abstract rightness or wrongness of particular terrorist acts or counter-terrorist measures than in what they accomplish and for what interests. They judge actions in terms of their consequences. Consider the case of terrorist acts by a committed group in the name of a worthy goal such as overthrowing a rapacious dictator. Or consider state terrorist measures employed to defeat a monstrous and clever political sect. Might not the end be worth the means? Would not a few deaths and a time of fear among certain people result in a much safer and freer outcome for the majority? Is that not a good moral bargain?

Obviously we cannot know the future, so consequentialist moral reasoning works better in hindsight than in prospect. The sociologist Barrington Moore argues that the death and suffering of the French Revolution, including the Terror, had the beneficent consequence of destroying social institutions of inequality and exploitation that were day after

---

Justifying civilian casualties

Rumsfeld said that despite the Pentagon's best efforts, civilian casualties are unavoidable.

'We have to know that there are going to be people hurt. Overwhelmingly, they will be people who we intend to hurt,' he said. 'On occasion there will be people hurt that one wished had not been. I don't think there is any way in the world to avoid that and defend the United States from the kinds of terrorist attacks which we've experienced.'

John Diamond, *Chicago Tribune*, 16 October 2001.

---

day grinding millions of lives into pain, despair and death. He judged this a good bargain from a long-term historical point of view.[7] Yet such judgments are hard to make, even historically. Judging events and actions before their consequences are known is much trickier still. The value of a judgment based on highly uncertain predictions is obviously compromised. Yet political leaders have to make such judgments all the time.

Political leaders are powerfully drawn to consequentialist moral reasoning on many policy issues. Damming a river harms some people and even destroys ways of life, but it helps others. The politicians in charge evaluate the balance of benefits and costs – no doubt giving special weight to influential power-holders and to the impact on their own careers. The same kind of reasoning can be applied to the distribution of violence. War planners try to deliver damage and death to enemy forces in the most efficient and effective pattern. They can and do also consider the benefits and costs of doing violence to civilians. Bombing Dresden will cause fire storms and kill tens of thousands of civilians. But perhaps it will demoralize the German high command, shorten the war and save the lives of allies and Germans alike. A suicide bomb in Tel Aviv will kill dozens of ordinary Israelis and trigger an Israeli attack on a West Bank refugee settlement that will kill Palestinians. But it will also recruit more suicide bombers and strengthen the radical Palestinian faction against the moderates and further the cause of restoring what is now Israel to the Palestinians. This is the way reasoning about the consequences of killing civilians justifies terrorist actions.

Consequentialist reasoning is used effectively against terrorism as well. Even in the case of terror or state terror that seems to promote benefits such as enhancing the power of a democratic state or weakening an evil government, opponents can argue that the consequences will be the creation of more enemies and the use of valuable resources needed elsewhere. This argument has been used by the Palestinian critics of suicide bombing and by opponents of the war on terrorism.

The consequentialist version of the terrorism debate often turns on the moral importance placed on enhancing state power. Machiavelli argued that the end of enhancing state power justifies the means of state violence against enemies and opponents who might otherwise weaken the state. For him, state power is more than an end in itself; it alone makes civic order and social morality practically possible. Those who support the power of a given state often follow Machiavelli's reasoning. They back the use of state terror as a regrettable necessity for solidifying state power and achieving the benefits the state brings over the long run. Those who oppose the extension of state power are often less critical of the terror of groups that attack the state because the damage people suffer looks small compared to the suffering the state inflicts.

Three big ideas
Debates about terrorism are colored by historical ideas as well as by moral standpoints. The ideas used

to explain terrorism often turn out to be connected to a vision of one of the big themes in our current history. There are three major themes here. Some familiarity with them helps in finding a way through the commentaries and debates that swirl around the war on terrorism. Each is in its own way too general and too weakly linked to any actual terrorist act to provide a full explanation of terrorism. At best each can give a partial insight into the context out of which terrorism emerges. But these ideas have another kind of importance – despite their weaknesses they guide the thought of planners of terrorist acts and of shapers of counter-terrorism policies.

Failed modernization. The most frequently-encountered big idea is failed modernization. The core idea here is that some societies have been unable to achieve the promise of growth in material wealth in a secular, science-based and democratic society. Two variants of the theme give it quite different interpretations. The neo-conservative variant argues that the opportunity to modernize is there for any society to seize. Countries like Taiwan, South Korea and Singapore provide examples of transformation into productive, relatively high-income market societies in a couple of generations. Failures are the responsibility of rulers and populations who did not take advantage of the opportunity to emulate the West by leapfrogging to the latest technologies. Persistent corruption, the wrong ideology, ancient conflicts or other misadventures have kept societies off the globalization train. Some fall into the abyss of failed or collapsed states unable to discharge even minimal government functions. The poverty and political instability that ensue breed frustration, calls for change, violence and even terrorism. They create conditions of urban anarchy and rural warlordism in which terrorists can gather, hide and prepare.

These neo-conservatives believe that even the richest of the developed economies and the most powerful

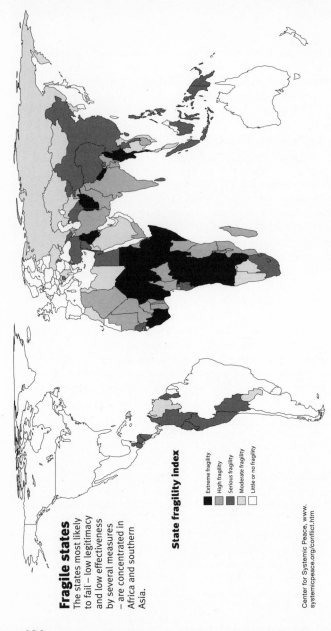

Fragile states

The states most likely to fail – low legitimacy and low effectiveness by several measures – are concentrated in Africa and southern Asia.

State fragility index

- Extreme fragility
- High fragility
- Serious fragility
- Moderate fragility
- Little or no fragility

Center for Systemic Peace, www.
systemicpeace.org/conflict.htm

political and military establishments cannot reverse or resolve all the failures of modernization. The best response is an agenda of self-protection – keeping the dangerous places under close scrutiny and going after terrorists when they appear. The governments of all countries, including those where terrorists gather, have a duty to crack down hard on these dangerous people.

The leftwing variant of failed modernization locates the weakness in the modernization model itself, which benefits rich countries at the expense of the poor. It simply does not fit the real possibilities of many countries, including large parts of Africa and the Middle East. The worst of the inequality, instability and poverty that breed and hide terrorists is remediable. The rich and powerful should reform the model of modernization and invest the money and effort needed to bring substantial benefits to the countries and regions most in need. This step will reduce the anger and frustration that breed terrorism, but action may still be necessary to deal with existing terrorist organizations.

Failed modernization, unfortunately for its proponents, itself fails to find the particular causes behind many episodes of terrorism. What about terrorism in paragons of modernization like Japan (Aum Shinrikyo) and Germany (Red Army Faction)? Why has Sri Lanka in recent years suffered from separatist terrorism and not Malaysia? Why are the crisis-ridden economies of the Caribbean less troubled by terrorism (state and group) than those of Central America? Modernization is in serious trouble, no question. But as a theory of terrorism it is too broad and vague. It stands in the way of understanding.

Clash of civilizations. A second way of seeing the big picture from which terrorism arises is the Clash of Civilizations, a phrase made famous from the titles of an article (1993) and a book (1996) by Samuel Huntington. The collapse of communism, according to this perspective, shifted the major lines of conflict in the world to the cultural. Supporters of this perspective find verification in Europe's Middle Ages when Muslim rule expanded into Spain and attempted to push into France, or when Christian crusades attempted to wrest control of Jerusalem from its Muslim rulers. But their main interest is the future: 'The dangerous clashes of the future are likely to arise from the interaction of Western arrogance, Islamic intolerance, and Sinic [Chinese] assertiveness,' says Huntington. The theory is elaborated from a frankly pro-Western perspective and designed to shape policy. The implication is that Westerners should expect recurring conflict with Islamic and Asian political powers. No amount of modernization will make 'them' more like 'us' and our observance of the values we regard as universal will not end the major differences.[8]

A variety of causes
Unfortunately, accepting the clash of civilizations as an organizing idea obscures insight into the actual variety of bases of terrorism. Cultural differences are without doubt an important source of conflict; but, so too are competition for resources like petroleum, water and land. Moreover, citizens, whatever their culture, are still stirred to vigorous opposition by experience with self-serving and corrupt concentrations of power that torture citizens and deny them basic rights. Differences of identity within the global cultures Huntington names, especially those stirred by nationalist claims, remain potent. The growing disparity of incomes within and between countries keeps ideologies of right and left alive in social movements. Among recent terrorist episodes, many have nothing to do with a clash of civilizations: the leftist claims of the Red groups in Europe; nationalist claims within a cultural zone of Basques in Spain, Kurds in Turkey and Tamils in Sri Lanka; the obscure rural revolutionary goals

of Sendero Luminoso in Peru; and the defense of the unborn by anti-abortion militants in the US. Cultural differences feed into political conflict, but to see terrorism through the lens of a clash of civilizations is a dangerous and blinding simplification.

Primary and secondary terrorism. A third perspective, put forward most coherently by Edward Herman and Gerry O'Sullivan in *The 'Terrorism' Industry*, focuses on state terrorism and downplays the importance and danger of group terrorism.[9] It locates the problem of terrorism in a large historical dynamic: the 'primary terrorism' of Western colonial expansion and continued economic and political domination provokes a 'secondary terrorism' of desperate response to the suffering and injustice inflicted by this primary terrorism. This analysis does not excuse or condone secondary terrorism, but it places historical responsibility for terrorist problems squarely in the hands of the Western perpetrators of primary terrorism. The historical causal force stimulating terrorist activity is Western expansionism and Western efforts to retain worldwide economic and political dominance. This perspective credits the claims often put forward by popular movements in the global South that the political settlements ending colonial rule were unjust and that post-colonial government is often the tool of Western economic and political interests. Its core equation is that the elimination of the injustices and relations of domination perpetrated by Western industrial powers will remove the raison d'être of terrorism.

This perspective captures one of the great waves of modern history that is too often neglected by writers looking at terrorism: the fundamental and often extreme violence of Western colonial expansion and the continuing resort to violence to retain post-colonial domination. It tends to ground itself on a few cases where evidence of US involvement in terrorism is strong, such as the mining of Nicaragua's harbor in support of Contra terrorism. But it makes no survey of a cross-section of terrorist acts and groups since the Second World War to see how well they fit the theory. It ignores the terrorism inside Europe from ETA in Spain to the Red Army Faction in Germany, but is markedly Euro- and US-centric when it comes to weighing the causes of terrorism in Latin America, Asia and Africa. It sees state terrorism in Brazil, Chile and Argentina and the Indonesian army slaughter in Timor Leste as the responsibility of the US. Is there no responsibility of those governments for their own actions?

Where the US failed to oppose state terrorism – even where it supported a security apparatus that engaged in such terrorism with money and training – there remains room for some moral and political autonomy on the part of 'client' governments. Governments that are in no way simple clients, like Myanmar (Burma) or Zimbabwe, are quite able to engage in state terrorism. Most former colonies and dependencies inherited an autocratic government and severe economic and political difficulties from their colonial experience, but terrorist regimes are prominent in only a few places. Nor can group terrorism automatically be traced to colonial violence and injustice. The idea of primary and secondary terrorism falls short as a general explanation of terrorism. Holding it too tightly stands in the way of understanding the many cases it fails to illuminate.

A less comprehensive theory of Western action and terrorist response is much more convincing with respect to specific cases and gives insight into the origins of state terrorism, a topic carefully ignored by many terrorism experts. It takes the name 'blowback', as noted in chapter three, from the term used inside the CIA for the unintended consequences of initial interventions. The US gave Saddam Hussein's regime in Iraq support to make it a stronger counterweight to Iran, but then President Hussein turned that power both against Iraq's Kurdish population and toward the invasion of Kuwait. The US gave assistance to the

Taliban via Pakistan's intelligence agency (and perhaps more directly) in order to strengthen a promising opponent of the Soviet occupation of Afghanistan. The Taliban succeeded admirably and turned its success to support of al-Qaeda and other Islamist terrorist organizations. These are just two cases where 'blowback' from US interventions resulted in terrorism turned against US interests.[10]

Because the needed information is highly controlled and manipulated and because the linkages between action and reaction involve many complex events and changing contexts, well-documented cases of blowback usually only come to light many years after the events. However, the fact that intelligence agencies themselves use the term shows that blowback is a persistent reality for insiders.[11]

Oddities of the moral-historical debate

Each of the above three perspectives paints the troubling terrorist episodes of the present on a much larger historical canvas. They appeal to existing prejudices and invite us to fit our understanding of today's terrorism into a familiar and comfortable formula. Their main function is to bolster a worldview that supports a broad policy stance with a combination of historical and moral-political interpretation. In their general forms they are of limited help in the task of understanding terrorism.

The neo-conservative idea of failed modernization suggests that Western policy can do nothing much of use for 'basket-case' countries. George Bush reflected that attitude during the election campaign in 2000. He replied to a question about assistance to Africa: 'I don't think nation-building missions are worthwhile.'[12] When basket cases are also incubators of terrorism requiring some kind of response, the main actions that are likely are military ones or counter-terrorism that tends to mimic the terrorism it opposes. Here again a wide-ranging historical theory limits policy ideas.

A deeper and more troubling issue is raised by the core idea of failed modernization: might modernization itself, even the seemingly successful type, sometimes breed discontents that can transmute into terrorism? Many terrorists are children of relative privilege offended by the inequalities, injustices and moral emptiness they connect with modernization. Their search for a cause beyond the normal politics of market society can set them on a path that leads to terrorism. Might it be that the bland power of self-satisfied market elites will always be provocative for the searching idealism of the young, drawing a few into a political calling that promises to be more exciting and morally grounded than any their society has on offer?

Some critics have argued that policy and rhetoric built on the idea of a clash of civilizations will tend to produce such a clash: the theory becomes self-fulfilling. The angry reaction in the Muslim world when President Bush called for a 'crusade' against terrorism confirms the danger of the symbolism of the Christian West versus Islam. The US leader never repeated that phrase and went out of his way to deny that Islam was in any sense the target or the enemy. Yet the phrase lingers on as an explanation for the pattern of US actions in the Middle East and in the war on terrorism.

Moralistic thinking can also narrow policy options and moralistic talk can undermine diplomatic efforts. People react where they see a whole nation or religion being called evil. They are also alienated when one government asserts a monopoly on the ability to define, perceive and defend universal human rights. A useful quality of consequentialist moral reasoning is that it forces the thinker to go beyond moral labeling to consider the social dynamics and end results of a particular action. The obligation to consider actual consequences can be very troubling to someone who wants simply to assert a categorical moral law or defend a moral community.

In the immediate aftermath of a terrorist attack, those harmed and aggrieved react as people wronged. They want their sense of violation to be shared, acknowledged and supported. Seeking to understand the grievances, motives and contexts out of which the attack might have grown is of no immediate interest to them. Even to raise such questions is offensive to many. After the attacks of 11 September, Americans who questioned the effectiveness of the US response were dismissed as America-haters and near traitors – even if they condemned the attacks as monstrous crimes. With the passage of time it has become less controversial to raise questions about the causes and contexts of frightful attacks.

The different forms of reasoning produced strange altercations over mentioning 'root causes' of terrorist attacks. For one-dimensional defenders of the US or Western moral community, even to think in this way was like finding excuses for the Devil's penchant for evil.

The US leaders who in the 'War on Terror' assert the categorical 'evil' of those they label terrorist adopt consequentialist reasoning about the actions of their own side. Thus defenders of the US bombing of Afghanistan acknowledge that many innocent civilians have been killed, but then point to the positive results of the military campaign: girls are now in school, children are vaccinated and food aid is getting through to hungry people. Moreover, they claim that they made extensive efforts to minimize civilian casualties. On balance, they argue, more citizens of Afghanistan are living and living freer and better than they would have been without the bombing.

Debate about such claims can be clarifying. Critics of the morality of bombing argue that civilian deaths are much more numerous than US officials admit and that unexploded bomblets and mines remain deadly dangers. They further claim that the new government is unstable and leaves known terrorist warlords in power to continue their terrorist ways. The gain in freedom for women is, they believe, overstated. They point to continuing general lawlessness and insecurity and to the return of Taliban control of much of the southern part of the country. The harvest of poppies and the export of heroin have resumed, once again to finance the Taliban and their allies. Such a debate covers matters that need to be investigated and taken into account in evaluating the military strategy in Afghanistan and in considering possible future action. But the argument is seldom joined in this manner. Each party tends to excuse its own violence against civilians using consequentialist reasoning while condemning the violence against its own civilians in terms of universal human rights or violation of a moral community.

From the perspective of making good policy choices that will minimize negative consequences, the case for examining contexts and causes is pragmatic and powerful. If terrorism is produced by a social process that can be analyzed, then to rid the world of terrorism, or even just to reduce its incidence, it makes sense to address these causes and contexts. Some leaders and commentators will get behind the emotional reflex to kill or punish the aggressors, but those who search a more considered response will *think* as well as feel. They will carefully weigh up the consequences of all possible retaliatory actions before they act.

The days that followed 11 September in the US are a telling example. The search for causes and consequences was scorned, at least publicly. An instant orthodoxy sprang to the lips of most leaders and commentators: al-Qaeda, Osama bin Laden and the Taliban had chosen the path of evil and had to be wiped out. The Afghan factions who fought alongside the Americans and who followed their established practice of 'bargaining' with the enemies were portrayed as moral cripples. But a more consequentialist approach would raise questions about why the enemy engages in terrorism and how they might be induced to abandon that path. It obliges the analyst to pursue kinds of understanding that do not start with simple moral invocation. It would raise questions of history, organization, leadership and social dynamics. Such questions lead to a kind of thinking that goes beyond just condemning terrorism to treating it as a social phenomenon that needs to be understood. This is the domain of military thinkers, policy analysts and social scientists who claim membership in the small group – the 'terrorism specialists'. Several centers and institutes have gathered and organized useful information about terrorism and, as the next chapter shows, the best of the analysts have developed some interesting ideas.

1 RG Frey and Christopher W Morris, *Violence, Terrorism, and Justice*, ed RG Frey, Cambridge Studies in Philosophy and Public Policy, Cambridge University Press, 1991. **2** Frantz Fanon, *The Wretched of the Earth*, Grove Press, 1963. **3** Richard F Grimmett, 'Authorization For Use Of Military Force in Response to the 9/11 Attacks (PL107–40): Legislative History', Order Code RS22357, by Richard F Grimmett, CRS Report for Congress (updated 16 January 2007). **4** Eleanor Acer, Eric Biel, Déirdre Clancy et al, *Assessing the New Normal: Liberty and Security for the Post-September 11 United States*, Lawyers Committee for Human Rights, 2003: 49–72, www.lchr.org. For updates on court cases see: www.humanrightsfirst. org. **5** David Rose, 'Neo Culpa', *Vanity Fair*, 3 November 2006. www. vanityfair.com **6** Michael Ignatieff, 'Getting Iraq Wrong', *The New York Times* magazine, 5 August 2007. **7** Barrington Moore, Jr, *Social Origins of Dictatorship and Democracy: Lord and Peasant in the Making of the Modern World*, Beacon Press 1966. **8** For citation sources see Robert Kaplan, 'Looking the World in the Eye', *Atlantic Monthly*, December 2001. **9** Edward Herman and Gerry O'Sullivan, *The 'Terrorism' Industry: The Experts and Institutions That Shape Our View of Terror*, Pantheon Books 1989. **10** Mahmood Mamdani, *Good Muslim, Bad Muslim: America, the Cold War, and the Roots of Terror*, Pantheon Books 2004. **11** Chalmers Johnson, *Blowback: The Costs and Consequences of American Empire*, Henry Holt 2000. **12** Presidential Debate at Wake Forest University, 11 October 2000.

5 Between politics and war

Terrorism operates in a dangerous no man's land where distinction between civilians and soldiers, authority and coercion, and politics and war lose their meaning. It is vital for counter-terrorist strategies to maintain the distinction and to preserve, enlarge and strengthen the reach of politics. The recent and novel formation of transnational terrorist networks with global ambitions makes a politically oriented response to terrorism both more difficult and more urgent.

MOST OF THE world has long noticed the existence of a fundamental global economic asymmetry between North and South going back decades. But with the demise of the Soviet Union, new asymmetries have become evident. The varying capacity of governments to retain authority and carry out basic state tasks gained attention as several countries became known as 'failed states'. Military inequality is unmistakable when no country can challenge the supremacy in conventional fighting capacity that the US invests in so heavily. The economic, political and military asymmetries are the source of serious tensions that are intensified by rapid global change, often summarized in the term 'globalization'. Goods, services, people, money, cultural creations, technical and scientific innovations and all manner of social organizations extend and move across national borders in increasing numbers and accelerated frequencies. The need for a global perspective is strikingly evident when it comes to the earth's warming climate and the dwindling supplies of fossil fuels. How terrorism fits into this world of change and stress is a preoccupation for military and political thinkers and actors. The war on terrorism initiated by the US Government in response to the attacks in New York and Washington in 2001 has brought the issues raised by military thinkers to the forefront.

Asymmetric warfare. Well-connected analysts had already been looking hard at the implications of asymmetry for US defense posture. They call into question almost every part of the defense establishment: training, tanks and other equipment, division into services, size and type of operational units and communications systems. Most importantly they propose a new doctrine to govern the changed art of war. They call it 'asymmetric warfare' or 'fourth generation warfare'.

The new doctrine asserts that terrorism is a new kind of enemy, one that is detached from state structures and devoid of conventional military weapons and tactics. All big industrial powers have military machines that are overwhelmingly more powerful than any terrorist group. Terrorism cannot threaten their military superiority. The danger of terrorism for the big powers is economic and political disruption. The complex integration of advanced economies and communications makes them vulnerable to attacks on such key elements as energy supplies, financial networks, information systems, population concentrations and symbols of national pride. Disruption is not military defeat, but it jolts the economy, tarnishes the reputation of the government of the day and interferes with its ability to extend its economic and cultural influence around the world. The governments of big powers are making major efforts to do something about the risks of terrorism. The question is: what can they do? Experts in asymmetric warfare think they have the answer in a new military posture, but a close look at their reasoning suggests an alternative response.

Their analysis looks beyond the military balance to the social and political map of the world. It draws on the ideas of failed modernization and cultural conflict discussed in chapter four. It goes something like this: In a world marked by extreme economic inequality and rapid social change, cultural friction ignites movements with extreme religious and political claims that sometimes turn to terrorism. Such non-state movements challenge and sometimes destroy the integrity and stability of weaker states and they can evolve into transnational terrorist organizations. International groups, notably al-Qaeda, may draw energy from local conflicts, but they operate internationally and pursue transnational goals. Al-Qaeda's mission is the kind the North's military planners worry about most. It wants to forge a new political unity for Islam, reshape political control of the oil-rich Middle East and weaken the power and ambition of the industrial North, particularly the US.

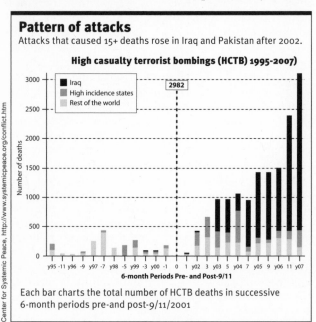

Pattern of attacks

Attacks that caused 15+ deaths rose in Iraq and Pakistan after 2002.

High casualty terrorist bombings (HCTB) 1995-2007

Legend:
- Iraq
- High incidence states
- Rest of the world

2982

Number of deaths (y-axis): 0, 500, 1000, 1500, 2000, 2500, 3000

6-month Periods Pre- and Post-9/11 (x-axis): y95, -11, y96, -9, y97, -7, y98, -5, y99, -3, y00, -1, 0, 1, y02, 3, y03, 5, y04, 7, y05, 9, y06, 11, y07

Each bar charts the total number of HCTB deaths in successive 6-month periods pre-and post-9/11/2001

Center for Systemic Peace, http://www.systemicpeace.org/conflict.htm

The social asymmetry that worries the military planners is concentrated in sprawling cities of the South like Karachi and Jakarta, lawless zones like northeastern Pakistan and whole countries such as Lebanon and Somalia marked by endemic conflict involving externally-funded terrorist groups. Iraq and Afghanistan are now on the list because invasion and occupation designed to eliminate terrorists have instead created new nodes of terrorist recruitment and training while failing to establish effective national governments.[1] Such places are crowded with young, diverse, underemployed populations with minimal government control. Here movements capable of terrorism find a supportive environment to recruit and train followers. A clandestine trade in weapons, drugs and cash opens the way for terrorists to act both locally and globally.

Since 2001 it has become evident that terrorist training and organization do not require failed states or lawless zones. Cities in Europe and North America can be good places for finding and forming recruits to terrorist networks. The very strengths of the industrial democracies can be used to the advantage of terrorists operating globally. Terrorists can use the freedom of information, movement, communication, education and acquisition to orchestrate terrorist attacks. Mohamed Atta, reputed to have headed the terrorist team that led the 11 September assault took full advantage of the freedom to meet, communicate and travel that he found in Hamburg to plan the attacks. American society was wide open to anyone wanting to learn basic flying skills. For military planners civil rights are a handicap in the war on terrorism.

Technical innovations add to the scope for terrorist action. Cell phones and the internet make transnational co-ordination easier. Computer programs for acquiring, storing, communicating, encrypting and organizing all kinds of information can be purchased. Flight simulating programs turn a notebook computer into a device for learning to fly. Newer explosives are more powerful for their weight and more easily handled and detonated. Terrorists learn from experience and search out new kinds of vulnerability in the societies they want to attack. The counter-terrorist thinkers say that terrorist actions have become more destructive in the last few years. There were a rising number of deaths per incident even before September 2001, although the number of incidents was declining.

The theorists emphasize that the greatest danger is that terrorists will get their hands on the very weapons that buttress the military superiority of the strong states: nuclear, biological and chemical weapons capable of harming whole cities or regions. Al-Qaeda's leaders, reports say, were trying to acquire chemical and biological weapons and had an interest in nuclear weapons and considered crashing a bomb-filled airplane into a nuclear reactor. And there was Aum Shinrikyo's faulty release of Sarin nerve gas in the Tokyo subway. Ready access to international travel, communication and technical information and the spread of engineering skills – all aspects of globalization – make it impossible to confine the capacity to use nuclear, biological, and chemical weapons to the big powers.

Looking into the future, the military analysts see the expansion of economically-polarized, culturally-splintered and politically-ungoverned zones throughout the global South. They note the large populations in Europe of immigrants from North Africa and the Middle East, some of whom are receptive to the idea of violent action in defense of Islam. They cite recent research showing that preexisting connections and friendships among young men are often the key to recruitment to terrorist groups that may lack effective hierarchical organization, but that share identification with a deeply-felt grievance against a common enemy. They notice that terrorist groups are becoming increasingly autonomous from any state sponsor and able to combine transnational linkages with locally-autonomous cells. Their weapons, it is feared, are likely to gain in destructive power and to be directed more frequently against strategic targets. They will also make increasingly effective use of mass media to spread fear, panic and confusion. If their picture is correct, the forecast by the leading hawks in and around the US Government who foresee and call for never-ending war seems well founded. Even the best intelligence with flexible and specially-trained forces and mobile equipment cannot realistically hope to put an end to the growing danger.

A different reading. Fortunately there is another way of reading the analysis of asymmetric warfare. Military specialists tend to take the asymmetric evolution of the globe as an unalterable given – a fact of nature. Their job is to devise a military solution to the problem it poses. However, the asymmetric conditions they emphasize are neither inevitable nor facts of nature; they are the outcome of policies and actions driven by the very countries most exercised by the terrorist danger. The theory of asymmetric warfare sees a collapse of distinctions between battlefield and homeland, soldier and civilian, combat and politics. The conventional conclusion is to broaden the notion of enemy, expand the field of warfare and develop ways of attacking and killing small groups, even individuals, anywhere in the world. The US is perfecting and implementing new technologies of information-gathering and imaging. The drones reported to have killed a wanted al-Qaeda member and four companions in Yemen in November 2002, and those that killed al-Qaeda members and civilians in Bajaur Agency, Pakistan, in January 2006, exemplify the new military doctrine in action.[2] Military targets must be broadened and military capabilities made more flexible. The society at home must accept new forms of surveillance and be kept on constant alert. In short, military thinking must colonize more and more of the political space.

A few analysts look at the same picture and draw a very different conclusion:

> If these or similar [political and economic] factors are indeed driving the evolution of conflict, then solutions must lie primarily in this arena, that is within the realms of economics, diplomacy, and law-enforcement. Military force will play a smaller role, performing specific tasks to solve problems that are intractable through other means. A coherent 'grand strategy' is needed to ensure that military (destructive) actions

---

Drones of death
1 Bush takes the law into his own hands

Zap! Pow! The bad guys are dead. And they never knew what hit them. ...George Bush etched another notch in his gun butt this week, blowing away six 'terrorists' in Yemen's desert. Their car was incinerated by a Hellfire missile, fired by a CIA unmanned aerial vehicle (UAV) or drone. Dealing out death via remote-controlled flying robots could be the spooks' salvation after the September 11 and Afghan intelligence flops. It makes the agency look useful. It is quick and bodybag-free...

It is, at best, irresponsible extra-judicial killing, at worst a premeditated, cold-blooded murder of civilians. And it is also, and this is no mere afterthought, morally unsustainable. Those who authorized this act have some serious ethical as well as legal questions to answer. That there is no prospect at all that they will, and no insistence by Britain or others that they do so, only renders ever more appalling the moral pit which gapes and beckons.

Zap! Crunch! So where next for the drones of death?... Stateless, gangster terrorism is a fearsome scourge. But state-sponsored terrorism is a greater evil, for it is waged by those who should know better, who are duty-bound to address causes not mere symptoms, who may claim to act in the people's name. As Alexander Herzen said in another age of struggle: 'We are not the doctors. We are the disease.'

Guardian Unlimited, 6 November 2002.

harmonize with our overall objectives and do not provoke a backlash that negates tactical success. Technology is not unimportant, and may provide options, but the fact is that lack of suitable technology cannot explain our less-than-stellar track record in fourth generation warfare.[3]

There are two assertions here with profound implications. The first is that a prevalent kind of terrorism cannot be defeated militarily. It has no state sponsors and therefore is less vulnerable to military strikes. Moreover, since it espouses causes that are gaining legitimacy in the eyes of many, military strikes will provoke a dangerous political backlash. Therefore, war on terrorism can hardly be 'fought' in a military sense and certainly cannot be 'won.' The

---

2 Al-Qaeda aims at Pakistan's heart

Prior to 2003, the entire al-Qaeda camp in the North Waziristan and South Waziristan tribal areas of Pakistan was convinced that its battle should be fought in Afghanistan against the foreign troops there, and not in Pakistan against its Muslim army.

That stance was changed by Sheikh Essa... in the town of Mir Ali in North Waziristan, where his sermons raised armies of takfiris (those who consider all non-practicing Muslims to be infidels). He was convinced that unless Pakistan became the Taliban's (and al-Qaeda's) strategic depth, the war in Afghanistan could not be won... On the advice of Sheikh Essa, militants have tried several times to assassinate [President] Musharraf, launched attacks on the Pakistani military, and then declared Bhutto a target.

This nest of takfiris and their intrigues was on the radar of the US Central Intelligence Agency (CIA) and the day after Bhutto's killing Sheikh Essa was targeted by CIA Predator drones in his home in North Waziristan. According to *Asia Times* Online contacts, he survived, but was seriously wounded...

This somewhat dampened the jubilation in the jihadi camps over Bhutto's death and al-Qaeda members had to flee to safe havens. Nevertheless, their intention to carry out more attacks is as steadfast as ever.

Syed Saleem Shahzad, *Asia Times*, 1 January 2008, www.atimes.com

second assertion is that the conditions that give rise to terrorism and make it such a difficult enemy can be altered through diplomatic, economic and political action. Here is room and reason to move away from seeing terrorism as mainly a military problem to seeing it as, in large part, a social/economic/political one. On a global scale it means addressing some of the great issues of modernization and globalization gone wrong.

A third theme can be added to this alternative reading of the theory of asymmetric warfare. The usual analysis exaggerates the danger posed by terrorism to the big industrial countries. The quick recovery from the destruction of such an important hub of financial transactions and information exchange as the World Trade Center shows that the system is less vulnerable than feared. The economy of Sri Lanka survived when the LTTE bombed the country's central bank and financial center. Pipelines, oil tankers and fuel depots have been targeted by terrorists in Colombia, the Persian Gulf and Israel without much impact on energy supply. Nuclear weapons are another matter, but lumping them together with biological and chemical weapons in the term 'weapons of mass destruction' disguises the very different dangers these weapons represent.

Nuclear weapons are by far the most destructive and by far the least likely to be used by terrorists. Scenarios of terrible attacks using chemical weapons can be imagined, but dispersal is quite difficult and its scope is likely to be limited. Biological weapons are potentially self-propagating, but their use will be discouraged by the fact that they also endanger the people they are meant to help or to avenge. Appallingly destructive attacks are possible, but disasters like Bhopal (4,000 dead, hundreds of thousands injured in a chemical leak in 1984) and the HIV/AIDS pandemic (in politically stable Botswana over 35 per cent of sexually active adults test positive) show that even poor societies often cope, if painfully, with chemical and biological disasters.

The symbolism and the psychological impact of terrorist attacks seems more telling than their economic effect. Bigger airplanes, office buildings and stadiums offer terrorists larger and symbolically more attractive targets. Chemical and biological agents and 'dirty bombs' could bring nightmares to waking life. But the prospect that they will gain the changes in power and politics the terrorists seek is vanishingly remote. The counter-terrorism track that gets the most publicity and investment offers little hope of real success, however. It amounts to the continuing militarization of matters better treated as social and political.

Local roots

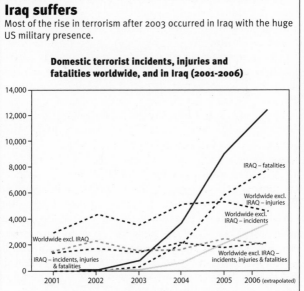

Iraq suffers

Most of the rise in terrorism after 2003 occurred in Iraq with the huge US military presence.

Domestic terrorist incidents, injuries and fatalities worldwide, and in Iraq (2001-2006)

Calculated by Jerry Mark Silverman from statistics in The National Memorial Institute for the Prevention of Terrorism (MIPT), 'Terrorism Knowledge Base' at www.mipt.org.

Between politics and war

A closer look at terrorism in operation confirms the importance of its political side. All terrorism is rooted in local contexts and the violence of all terrorist attacks occurs in distinct locales. Even the movements with global reach like al-Qaeda and Hizbullah began in a specific region and gave voice to particular grievances. It is true that terrorists like Abu Nidal or Carlos the Jackal became guns-for-hire willing to operate almost anywhere. But they get hired by movements or governments acting in a particular context. Most terrorist organizations emerge not in failed states or chaotic zones of bloated megacities but in countries with relatively stable governments: Ireland, Egypt, Spain, Algeria, Colombia, Sri Lanka, Italy and the US. These are not failed states, although some have become less stable under the impact of terrorism. The role of failed states and unstable zones – Lebanon, Palestine, Afghanistan and Iraq – is less as generators of terrorism than as places where terrorists may gather and gain practical experience against known enemies.

To understand terrorist organization we need to grasp how it connects with the local context. Knowing the social background of terrorist activists provides important clues. Take two examples:

In the year that President Nasser hanged Sayyid Qutb, the writer and activist who advocated replacing Egypt's Arab socialism with an Islamist state, a 15-year-old boy from a family of prominent Cairo doctors and educators founded a secretive group in his high school devoted to keeping Qutb's ideas alive and working to overthrow Nasser's Government. The year was 1966 and the boy was Ayman al-Zawahiri, later to merge the Egyptian Islamic Jihad with Osama bin Laden's al-Qaeda organization and to become the chief strategist and organizational manager of al-Qaeda. The Egyptian dissident sociologist, Saad Eddin Ibrahim, who has studied Islamist activists in his country, explains that typically they are 'model Egyptians' from educated middle class families. The parents are often government bureaucrats or professionals. Al-Zawahiri once bragged to a visiting American that most of the members of his Islamist group were from the elite university faculties of medicine and engineering.[4]

Abimael Guzmán Reymoso, founder and leader of Sendero Luminoso in Peru until his arrest in 1992, was, as a middle class university student in the mid-1960s, drawn to Marxist thought and revolutionary action. He was moved by the plight of the poor and landless peasantry of Ayacucho, where he taught philosophy. He explained to his captors in 1992, 'Their reality shook my eyes and my mind.' Already as a student he had found compelling the writings of José Carlos Mariátegui, a founder of Peruvian socialist thought, and Stalin, whom he called 'a great Marxist-Leninist, a great man' despite his 'mistakes.' Based on his own version of peasant-based revolutionary communism Guzmán initiated a guerrilla and terrorist conflict in 1980 that lasted a dozen years and killed an estimated 30,000 Peruvians in a brutal cycle of terrorism and counter-terrorism. Most of those who died were the poor peasants in whose name Guzmán launched his struggle.[5]

If the leaders of terrorist organizations are often from the middle class, many of the rank and file members come from poorer and rougher backgrounds in the refugee camps, shanty towns and neglected countryside. Groups of friends, co-members of sports teams, or kin-related youth may together adhere to a movement or come under the influence of a recruiter. The social service side that is a vital part of some terrorist organizations has a presence in places where unemployment is more common than employment. Along with social services they provide an explanation of the surrounding misery and the promise of a disciplined approach to doing something meaningful.

The large nationalist movements recruit widely from the popular classes. The parties to violence in Ireland like the Catholic Provisional IRA and the Protestant Ulster Volunteer Force draw from the working class. The FARC in Colombia, LTTE in Sri Lanka and Kurdistan Workers' Party (PKK) in Turkey attract activists from low-income rural and urban backgrounds.

Women and terrorism

Even the phrase 'women terrorists' heightens the sense of extremism and irrationality that is attached to terrorism. In the 1950s people were shocked when women members of the Algerian FLN planted bombs in cafes and cinemas during the campaign against French rule. The idea of women or girls as suicide bombers is especially disturbing to many people. What are their motives? How are they indoctrinated? Such questions are rarely asked about men, as if terrorism and suicide missions are normal outlets for young male urges. Women are more frequently seen as mothers or wives, often gravely supporting the terrorist cause. Their most familiar role is that of victim, whether as casualties in indiscriminate attacks in public places or special targets for rape and physical abuse. Calls for action against terrorism often invoke the deaths of 'innocent women and children' as reason for harsh reprisals.

Yet women as leaders and warriors in terrorist groups are not unusual. Leila Khaled received international publicity and became a role model for her cool elegance in hijacking a TWA flight from Rome to Athens in 1969. The mission, her first for the Popular Front for the Liberation of Palestine, ended with all hostages released alive. Two armed women were among the four Palestinians who hijacked a Lufthansa flight from Majorca to Frankfurt in 1977. They demanded money and the freeing of Red Army Faction prisoners in Germany. One of the women was killed and the other wounded when a German anti-terrorist squad stormed the plane in Mogadishu.

Among the leaders of the Red Army Faction were two women, Ulrike Meinhof and Gudrun Ensslin. Women were well-represented among active members and leaders in the left wing terrorist organizations of Europe and North America. Many of them came to terrorism from university activism and many had family ties with other members of organizations that engaged in terrorism.

The Sociology and Psychology of Terrorism: Who Becomes a Terrorist and Why? US Library of Congress, Washington DC, September 1999.

The European and Japanese leftwing and anarchist terrorist groups of the 1970s, on the other hand, drew their members mainly from the middle class. Most of them had some university education; many began their activist career while in university. For example the Red Army Faction (also called the Baader-Meinhof Gang) included among its members Gudrun Ensslin, daughter of an evangelical church pastor; Suzanne Albrecht, daughter of a wealthy lawyer; Andreas

---

Robin Morgan, as an active member of the Weather Underground in the US, opposed the male dominance she encountered inside the group. From her own experience and a study of terrorism she concludes that 'the central knot of terrorism' is 'the intersection of violence, eroticism, and what is considered "masculinity".' To succeed, any action against terrorism must dethrone the idea of the violent, single-minded, controlling and self-sacrificing hero/martyr. Women too, she says, come under the enchantment of this idea and some willingly serve as helpers, supporters and lovers of terrorists. She and others believe that women have the compassion and vision to work against terrorism and the violence that is bound up with patriarchy. The Women's Peace Movement in Northern Ireland, Women in Black in Israel and Palestine, and mothers' clubs in Peru, for example, all work to end the violence of conflicts that include terrorism.

Robin Morgan, *The Demon Lover: The Roots of Terrorism*, Washington Square Press, 2001.

Women in state terrorism? They must be present somewhere, but the writing on state terrorism has little to say about them. Two recent items: American officials have found that assigning a female interrogator to a case can throw some [imprisoned al-Qaeda] suspects off-stride.

Eric Schmitt, 'There Are Ways to Make Them Talk', *New York Times*, 16 June 2002.

Zoria Shrfaei, head of the Algerian association for defending women's rights, stated that the number of women who were raped by terrorist groups reached 5,000, saying that statistics said that 1,313 women were raped between 1994 and 1997 and that more than 2,000 were kidnapped and killed in year 1997. In 1998 the Government opened the first center to take care of women raped by terrorists.

26 February 2000 and 19 October 1998, www.arabicnews.com

Baader, son of a historian; Ulrike Meinhof, daughter of an art historian; Horst Mahler, son of a dentist; and Holger Meins, son of a business executive.[6]

These cases confirm that the material grievances of the poorest and most exploited are not often the mainspring of terrorist action (although in anti-colonial violence and peasant uprisings landless peasants sometimes attacked settlers who had occupied their land). In itself poverty rarely imparts the emotional energy that is evident in acts of terrorism. The springs of terrorism lie rather in a sense of humiliation, degradation and disrespect. Poverty and exploitation are important as marks of the humiliation visited upon the people with whom one identifies. The commentators who assert that material suffering has nothing to do with terrorism because so many terrorists are middle-class simply fail to see that the connection between poor living conditions and political action passes through a feeling that the group with which one identifies is held in contempt. Poverty and exploitation are important as marks of humiliation and degradation.

In the case of suicide bombers who have become a favored terrorist weapon, the kind of personal experience that feeds the motivating anger or hatred is often physical or social humiliation inflicted upon a family member, a close associate or oneself. One of the mechanisms that keeps the cycle of terrorism and counter-terrorism going is the reciprocal and deliberate effort to humiliate the other side. According to leaders of Islamic Jihad, al-Qassam Brigades and Hamas there is no shortage of volunteers for suicide missions following an Israeli assault in the occupied territories. Hatred of the occupation is often compounded by the death or injury of friends by Israeli military action. Resistance actions are commemorated in 'revenge songs.' Thus by intention and by circumstance does the cycle of terrorism/counter-terrorism perpetuate itself.

Grievances and anger never lead directly to terrorist action. People, usually young people, have to be recruited to terrorism and their loyalty and obedience maintained. Local contexts and the immediate incentives are crucial here. Big forces of social dislocation have to feed into an effective local strategy for a terrorist organization to thrive. Enduring terrorist organizations become part of the local social landscape. They are one of the 'career choices' which local youth may adopt. Where employment is hard to find and career paths rare, terrorist activism may seem a viable choice. The terrorist entrepreneur with a knack for recruiting young men and women, much like the enthusiastic organizer of a youth club, often has a key role to play.

Many commentators remark on the charismatic appeal of Osama bin Laden and credit it for al-Qaeda's influence among dissatisfied Arab and Muslim youth. Local conflicts and the personal magnetism of recruiters combine with the particular adolescent angst of a young person or a group of young friends to produce success for terrorist entrepreneurs. An impressive terrorist attack and a repressive counter-terrorist response can trigger successful recruitment. The attack symbolizes the potency of the organization and its cause; the repression confirms the view that terror tactics are morally legitimate and practically necessary.

Organization

A terrorist organization must have a way of organizing and educating that confirms and retains the interest and commitment of new recruits. Terrorist organizations use several, often contradictory, methods for retaining loyalty. On the positive side are rituals that inspire feelings of camaraderie and belonging to a larger cause. The videotapes made by suicide bombers on the eve of their sacrificial violence express adherence to both cause and family. They convey the serenity of total commitment. Leaders, present and past, become heroes to emulate. Material support for recruits and their families lends recognition and may compensate in some part for the loss to a family of a lifetime of earnings by a son or a husband. The governments of Iran and Iraq, and wealthy Saudis are all reported to contribute to funds that make payments to the families of suicide 'martyrs'.

On the negative side, recruits can be kidnapped and pushed into actions that make them criminals wanted by the authorities. Fear keeps such recruits in line. The main purpose of a cell structure is to prevent the capture of any one member from unraveling more than a single cell in the larger organization. But it can also play a role in controlling lower-level recruits. The lack of horizontal communication among cells prevents recruits from talking to one another and sharing any grievances they may have. Threats and intimidation may neutralize any move against the local leadership.

Where an identity group is fighting for political autonomy and where terrorism has become part of an ongoing way of life – as in Northern Ireland, Palestinian refugee camps and Tamil towns and villages in northern Sri Lanka – terrorist organizations, like youth gangs in many western cities, are a powerful magnet for boys and girls approaching adulthood. Peer pressure, family tradition and exemplary heroes play a part in the choice made. Youth who do not abhor violence and who want to be true to the beliefs of their fathers and mothers will be drawn in. Their leaders know how to identify the best prospects and guide them into terrorist activity.

In the case of organizations defined by a political ideology like the Red Army Faction, the Red Brigades and the Weather Underground the path to terrorism is often quite different. Young people in the European or North American context may also be searching for meaning in their lives, but end up at odds with the social and political stance of the adult world including their parents. There are many accounts of better-off young people who, in a period of soul-searching about their future, come under the influence of a radical spokesperson or group that plots a convincingly different course for them. Typically the new course struggles against apparent and real injustices from which their inherited life plan would profit. Those who rebel have a sense that they are acting on principles that their parents hold only rhetorically. Young militants in a national struggle – as in Israel, Palestine, Northern Ireland, Basque country and Tamil country – work to revive a homeland that earlier generations were unable to defend. Or they may feel they are choosing commitments quite opposite to their parents' hated ideals, as was the case of some members of the Red Brigades in post-fascist Italy and the Red Army Faction in post-Nazi Germany.

State terrorist organizations have much larger budgets and accepted processes for recruiting, training and paying soldiers or hiring privately trained and managed security personnel. State-run proxy organizations in comparison to non-state groups are likely to give more importance to material incentives and less to ideology. Beliefs about identity and ideology can move government leaders just as they do group terrorist leaders. Their moral compass may justify attacks against both internal opponents and external enemies. Doctrines of national security, Nazism and communism can be shaped to persuade the rank and file of the need for terror tactics. One of the most common justifications for perpetrators of state terrorism is that they act in the name of counter-terrorism to defend the dignity and power of the state. Beneath the rhetoric, simply hanging onto power is often a major motive. The revered leader is often invoked as the 'great explainer' who assumes responsibility for the 'necessary' politics of terror.

Between politics and war

The art of shaping cadres of young people, usually men, into willing torturers and killers is well honed and well known to military establishments. The key is to unite a sense of larger mission (defending the nation) with a sense of group loyalty and interdependence (fighting for one's comrades). Armies have long been adept at such training, isolating the trainees from family and society and using boot-camp techniques to reinforce obedience to the chain of command and loyalty to a team of soldiers. The military and civilian managers of military operations are imbued with a belief in the strategic value of aggression and violence in the pursuit of certain national or regime interests. The very same combination of strategic aggression and group dependence has often been turned to purposes of state terrorism. The commander of a special unit need only declare that certain people are enemies of state security and the soldiers' license-to-kill can be directed against that group.

Philip Zimbardo's famous psychology experiment at Stanford University in 1971 that placed students in the roles of prisoners and guards in a simulated prison showed how rapidly ordinary young men could be turned toward torture. The experiments had to be ended abruptly after only six days because the 'guards' subjected the 'prisoners' to sadistic treatment. Zimbardo himself experienced a 'shock of recognition' on looking at the photographs of Americans abusing prisoners at Abu Ghraib Prison in Iraq. He has no doubt that normal, loyal, upstanding American soldiers can readily be placed in situations and given instructions where they abuse and torture others.[7] Forming state terrorists must follow a similar pattern.

The larger mission that cements state-terrorist resolve may be a nationalist ideology, but it may also be a sectional loyalty within a culturally segmented country. Many national leaders in poorly integrated countries are best seen as warlords with a sectional base who have seized national power. They may cement support in one region or one group while focusing repression on a region or a group represented as alien or disloyal. A skillful and ruthless leader like Saddam Hussein can direct a security service recruited from a favored group to undertake terrorist action against a vilified minority. Saddam Hussein's poison gas attack on the Kurdish population of Halabja in 1988 was also a warning to opponents in other regions of the punishment that might await them.[8]

Many participants in terrorist organizations become attached to the excitement of danger, secrecy and dissimulation. There is the rush of living outside the rules, getting away with doing what is forbidden. In the case of suicide bombers the cult of martyrdom and an acceptance of death in the name of a great cause are sufficient. State terrorists gain the sense of being part of the specially-formed 'professional' team authorized to use criminal violence for patriotic reasons.

Potential recruits and their families also may be making a rational calculus about how their security and wellbeing are most likely to be enhanced and least likely to be damaged. Their local worlds are penetrated by many kinds of division and conflict. It is not unusual for families to place sons in more than one local faction in order to hedge their bets and to preserve some useful contact with all parties. The complexity of the family ties and personal networks is sometimes surprising. Families knit connections on both sides of divisions that appear superficially to be unbridgeable.

Global outstretch
The military strategists of asymmetric warfare may overemphasize the globalization of terrorism, but they signal a real trend that US policy has inadvertently encouraged. Al-Qaeda was greatly strengthened when al-Zawahiri merged Egyptian Islamic Jihad with

Between politics and war

Osama bin Laden's group. Its recruits from dozens of countries shared the experience, supported by the US, of training and fighting in Afghanistan and forged a new kind of transnational identity for the organization. Intelligence experts believe it also had training centers in the Philippines and Indonesia. Its core was flexible enough to make use of the strengths of its branch operations.[9] It remained active and effective even after the US-led invasion drove al-Qaeda from its base in Afghanistan. Expert observers believe it lost much of its operational control and that the autonomy of groups elsewhere claiming allegiance was enhanced, while the leaders took refuge in the border region of Pakistan and Afghanistan. They

Terrorist acts causing death since September 2001 suspected of being carried out or inspired by al-Qaeda

- 2002 (April): Explosion at historic synagogue in Tunisia left 21 dead, including 11 German tourists.
- 2002 (May): Car exploded outside hotel in Karachi, Pakistan, killing 14, including 11 French citizens.
- 2002 (June): Bomb exploded outside American consulate in Karachi, Pakistan, killing 12.
- 2002 (Oct): Boat crashed into oil tanker off Yemen coast, killing 1.
- 2002 (Oct): Nightclub bombings in Bali, Indonesia, killed 202, mostly Australian citizens.
- 2002 (Nov): Suicide attack on a hotel in Mombasa, Kenya, killed 16.
- 2003 (May): Suicide bombers killed 34, including 8 Americans, at housing compounds for Westerners in Riyadh, Saudi Arabia.
- 2003 (May): 4 bombs killed 33 people targeting Jewish, Spanish, and Belgian sites in Casablanca, Morocco.
- 2003 (Aug): Suicide car-bomb killed 12, injured 150 at Marriott Hotel in Jakarta, Indonesia.
- 2003 (Nov): Explosions rocked a Riyadh, Saudi Arabia, housing compound, killing 17.
- 2003 (Nov): Suicide car-bombers simultaneously attacked 2 synagogues in Istanbul, Turkey, killing 25 and injuring hundreds.
- 2003 (Nov): Truck bombs detonated at London bank and British consulate in Istanbul, Turkey, killing 26.
- 2004 (March): 10 bombs on 4 trains exploded almost simultaneously

retain a powerful symbolic presence issuing frequent admonitions to followers and warnings to enemies. The new decentralized al-Qaeda is judged by many experts to be more dangerous than ever.[10] A long list of attacks since 11 September 2001 is attributed to al-Qaeda.

The US, as the leader of the war on terrorism, tries to globalize counter-terrorism by drawing governments into a common policy of military and police action against terrorists of all stripes. Governments are pressed to enact tough security legislation and to crack down on groups suspected of international connections. Often, as in the case of Indonesia, they are given military assistance and military training.

---

during the morning rush hour in Madrid, Spain, killing 191 and injuring more than 1,500.

• 2004 (May): Terrorists attacked Saudi oil company offices in Khobar, Saudi Arabia, killing 22.

• 2004 (June): Terrorists kidnapped and executed American Paul Johnson, Jr., in Riyadh, Saudi Arabia.

• 2004 (Sept): Car bomb outside the Australian embassy in Jakarta, Indonesia, killed 9.

• 2004 (Dec): Terrorists entered the U.S. Consulate in Jeddah, Saudi Arabia, killing 9 (including 4 attackers).

• 2005 (July): Bombs exploded on 3 trains and a bus in London, England, killing 52.

• 2005 (Oct): 22 killed by 3 suicide bombs in Bali, Indonesia.

• 2005 (Nov): 57 killed at 3 American hotels in Amman, Jordan.

• 2006 (Jan): Two suicide bombers carrying police badges blew themselves up near a celebration at the Police Academy in Baghdad, killing nearly 20 police officers. Al-Qaeda in Iraq took responsibility.

• 2007 (April): Suicide bombers attacked a government building in Algeria's capital, Algiers, killing 35 and wounding hundreds more. Al-Qaeda in the Islamic Maghreb claimed responsibility.

• 2007 (April): 8 people, including 2 Iraqi legislators, died when a suicide bomber struck inside the Parliament building in Baghdad. An organization that includes al-Qaeda in Mesopotamia claimed responsibility. In another attack, the Sarafiya Bridge that spans the Tigris River was destroyed.

Adapted from www.infoplease.com

Between politics and war

Sometimes, as in the Philippines and Somalia, the US supports co-operative governments with troops as well as economic assistance.

The War on Terror gives al-Qaeda, and terrorism in general, a strong global image. States facing any kind of insurgency claim that they are a fighting the global

Anti-terrorism laws and human rights

1 UK: Human rights: a broken promise

Since 11 September 2001, the UK authorities have passed a series of new laws [with] sweeping provisions that contravene human rights law, and their implementation has led to serious abuses of human rights.

People suspected of involvement in terrorism... have been... held for years in harsh conditions on the basis of secret accusations that they are not allowed to know and therefore cannot refute.

Amnesty International 2006, Index Number: EUR 45/004/2006, www.amnesty.org

2 Anti-terrorism legislation curbs media's freedom of expression

Overly vague and broad definitions of 'terrorism' are too often used to arrest and intimidate journalists, detain protesters and target political dissidents in the name of security. These actions are justified by the so-called global 'war on terror'...

Illustratively, in Sri Lanka... anti-terrorism legislation is used to silence media, particularly those reporting on Tamil issues or disseminating Tamil-language news. The spokesperson and financial director of Standard Newspapers Private Ltd., Dushantha Basnayake, was arrested in February 2007 under the Prevention of Terrorism Act (PTA 2002). Alleged to have links with the Liberation Tigers of Tamil Eelam (LTTE), Basnayake remains detained without charge. The company has since had its assets frozen and been closed down...

In Uganda Kizza Besigye, President Museveni's political foe, continues to be detained under charges of treason and terrorism. While in exile for four years, he appeared regularly on a popular Ugandan radio show. For this the show was routinely threatened with prosecution under the Anti-Terrorism Act 2002. Threats were extended to anyone seen to be 'spreading propaganda' and supporting Besigye...

In Kenya in 2007 despite having all clearance and the proper documentation, a British journalist and his colleague were arrested and questioned on the pretext of being suspected terrorists merely for filming the outside of a police station as part of a documentary on the arrest and deportation of Islamists.

terrorist enemy. Russia puts Chechen separatists in this category, in order to garner international support and legitimacy, especially from the US. Some Chechen insurgents find it useful to adopt the garb of radical Islam and deliver videotaped messages to al Jazeera television. Like other local movements they are drawn

Sophie Earnshaw, Commonwealth Human Rights Initiative, 2 May 2007, http://southasia.oneworld.net

3 Amnesty International is concerned that the USA Patriot Act:

• Creates a broad definition of 'domestic terrorism' that may have a chilling effect on the U.S. and international rights to free expression and association.

The law defines 'domestic terrorism' as acts committed in the United States 'dangerous to human life that are a violation of the criminal laws,' if the US Government determines that they 'appear to be intended' to 'influence the policy of a government by intimidation or coercion,' or 'to intimidate or coerce a civilian population.' Such ambiguous language allows for loose interpretation that might violate civil liberties and international human rights.

• Allows non-citizens to be detained without charge and held indefinitely once charged.

This is permissible if the US Government certifies that there are 'reasonable grounds' to believe a person's action threatens national security. This runs counter to US and international rights to due process and could also lead to violations of rights in the Vienna Convention on Consular Relations, which guarantee that governments be notified if their nationals are detained.

• Infringes on the right to privacy and removes many types of judicial review over intelligence activities.

The USA PATRIOT Act permits the government to scrutinize people's reading habits by monitoring public library and bookstore records, without notifying the suspect. It also allows for 'sneak and peak' tactics such as physical search of property and computers, wiretapping and monitoring of email, and access to financial and educational records, without providing notification. These activities contradict the right to be free from arbitrary interference with individuals' privacy, as protected in the US Constitution and the ICCPR.

Amnesty International USA, 2007,
www.amnestyusa.org/War_on_Terror/Civil_Rights

to represent themselves as part of a global endeavor in order to gain publicity and international support for their cause. Facing a common enemy, diverse locally-based movements move to enhance their collaboration.

What the war on terrorism does

For governments the war on terror fills a void that appeared with the end of the Cold War and the spread of neo-conservative views that governments should shrink and scale back their programs. It gives governments something important to do and supplies a ready reason to strengthen instruments of internal security and to monitor or restrict potentially troublesome political movements.

The fight against communism or imperialism was reason enough in Cold War days for governments to expand their power. With the demise of state communism the US reduced support for repressive anti-communist regimes. Democracy movements and competitive politics spread widely in the unipolar world. Democratic movements are often disrespectful of sitting governments and they can generate conflict that brings political order itself into question. Many governments discovered reasons to fear democracy. The war on terrorism gives them the opportunity to play on the widely-felt sense of vulnerably to reinforce their power. Governments the world over are beefing up police and intelligence agencies and implementing legislation that curtails political liberties and reduces protection against arbitrary arrest.

The war on terrorism draws attention away from issues of global inequality and degradation of living conditions that are important in their own right and remain important causes of conflict. Instead international bodies are swamped by issues of security. The global movement for economic reform finds its scope for action more limited. In the industrial North it finds governments are less open to discussion about economic justice. The public is encouraged to see the South more as a source of danger than a region in need of international economic and social reform. Activists have to commit energy and resources to defending human and civil rights and opposing the worst of the new security legislation. A coalition that might come together on many aspects of global economic reform and environmental defense is more divided when forced into dealing with issues of security and terrorism.

Debate about globalization is being choked off at a time when a new generation of activists is responding to the changing constellation of power and wealth in the world and participating in vital cultural changes and conflicts. Lively debates are underway on fundamental issues such as the political role of Islam, Christianity and Judaism; appropriate political structures for multicultural states and alternatives to orthodox market solutions to issues of stalled development and income maldistribution. These debates need wide publicity and broad participation.

Liberal secularists need to debate why modernization is failing so many of the world's people. Instead they are caught up in arguing about the morality of investing heavily in weapons. Religious believers need to discuss how they can adapt their beliefs to a pluralism of faiths but instead are forced to defend their religion's basic morality.

The politics of fear and power replaces a politics of intellectual challenge and practical give and take. The war on terrorism includes a well-funded and skillfully-directed information component that raises the fear level and keeps attention on security. It sucks energy from other discussions and forces basic issues to the margins of public dialog. The way the war on terrorism enables the US to shape the political agenda within the US, in international discussions and in many other countries may be its most impressive quality.

Dislocation

The war on terrorism also draws attention away from arms control and arms elimination projects. Efforts to reduce the availability of land mines, light automatic weapons and explosives might have a direct effect on the frequency and deadliness of terrorist actions. Control of the production and distribution of nuclear, biological and chemical weapons would lower the chances of terrorists making use of such weapons. These efforts are weakened and displaced by enlarged military budgets and accelerated production of weapons systems for possible counter-terrorist use.

Wars can bring an end to state terrorist regimes. The Allies defeated Nazi Germany, Vietnam terminated the Pol Pot regime in Cambodia, Tanzania overthrew the government of Idi Amin in Uganda, and the RPF defeated the genocidal rulers of Rwanda. Group terrorists are not readily defeated militarily. Good police work and the arrest of key leaders has weakened terrorist organizations. Over time leaders and causes wear down, age, and sometimes wither into weakness. In several cases local terrorist movements have decided to abandon their more extreme claims and enter a process of political bargaining. It takes a confident government to approach negotiations with the flexibility needed to stick with a process that will usually have major setbacks before it succeeds. Movements with a strong popular base that have sufficient democratic influence to hold the militants to account have the best prospects of trading terrorist attacks for political action. Political order will never totally remove the possibility of terrorism. From time to time in every country some people will abandon politics for terrorist violence. But to use our political and police skills to minimize terrorist actions is a realistic course of action.

The world will have to continue to live with terrorism. Governments and citizens can do a lot to limit its incidence. We badly need to curtail the damage it does to popular action and governmental work on the life and death political issues that face humankind.

1 'Study cites seeds of terror in Iraq. War radicalized most, probes find', *The Boston Globe*, 17 July 2005. 'Curbing terrorism stumbles over Bush's war on terror. Iraq desert becomes chief training ground for killing Americans', *San Francisco Chronicle*, 20 March 2005. **2** James Risen, 'Threats and Responses: Drone Attack', *New York Times*, 8 November 2002; Human Rights News, 'Pakistan: End Excessive Use of Force in Counter-terrorism Operations' New York, 1 November 2006, www.hrw.org **3** Defense and National Interest DNI, Created and managed by Kettle Creek Corp, Atlanta, GA, www.d-n-i.net/second_level/fourth_generation_warfare. htm **4** Lawrence Wright, 'The Man behind Bin Laden', *The New Yorker*, 22 September 2002. **5** World Affairs, Summer 1993 v156 n1 p52 (6) 'Exclusive' comments by Abimael Guzmán. From Foreign Broadcast Information Service, Latin America, 25 February 1993. 'Transcribed excerpts' of an 'exclusive' tape recording from a Dincote, Counter-terrorism Directorate, cell in Lima, 'last September'. **6** *The Sociology and Psychology of Terrorism: Who Becomes a Terrorist and Why?* A report prepared under an Interagency Agreement by the Federal Research Division, Library of Congress, September 1999, www.loc.gov/rr/frd/Sociology-Psychology **7** Philip Zimbardo, *The Lucifer Effect: How Good People Turn Evil*, Random House 2007. **8** Joost R Hiltermann, 'Halabja: America didn't seem to mind poison gas', *International Herald Tribune*, 17 January 2003, www.iht.com **9** Susan Schmidt and Douglas Farah, 'Six Militants Emerge From Ranks to Fill Void', *Washington Post*, 29 October 2002. **10** Marc Sageman, *Understanding Terror Networks*, University of Pennsylvania Press 2004.

Contacts

INTERNATIONAL
Amnesty International
Tel: +44 20 7413 5500
www.amnesty.org

The Counterterrorism Blog
http://counterterrorismblog.org

International Committee of the Red Cross
Tel: + 41 22 733 20 57
www.icrc.org

The International Institute for Strategic Studies (IISS)
Tel: +44 20 7379 7676
www.iiss.org

International Rehabilitation Council for Torture Victims
Tel: +45 33 76 06 00
Email: irct@irct.org   www.irct.org

UN Action Against Terrorism
Tel: +1 800 253 9646
www.un.org/terrorism

CANADA
Canadian Centre for Victims of Torture
Tel: +1 416 363 1066
www.ccvt.org

ISRAEL
Institute for Counter-Terrorism
Tel: +972 9 9527277
www.ict.org.il

SOUTH ASIA
South Asia Terrorism Portal
Email: icm@del3.vsnl.net.in
www.satp.org

UK
Oxford Research Group
Tel: +44 20 7549 0298
www.oxfordresearchgroup.org.uk

Peace Brigades
Tel: +44 20 7065 0775
www.peacebrigades.org

US
Federation of American Scientists
Tel: +1 202 546 3300
Email: fas@fas.org
www.fas.org/terrorism/index.html

GlobalSecurity.org
Tel: +1 703 548 2700
Email: info@globalsecurity.org
www.globalsecurity.org/index.html

Human Rights Watch
Tel: +1 212 290 4700
Email: hrwnyc@hrw.org
www.hrw.org

The Jamestown Foundation
Tel: +1 202 483 8888
www.jamestown.org/terrorism/index.php

Memorial Institute for the Prevention of Terrorism (MIPT)
Tel: +1 405 278 6300
www.mipt.org

The National Counter-terrorism Center (NCTC)
www.nctc.gov

National Security Archive
Tel: +1 202 994 7000
nsarchiv@gwu.edu

The Project on Defense Alternatives
Tel: +1 617 5474474
www.comw.org/pda/

The Rand Corporation
Tel: + 1 310 393 0411
www.rand.org/research_areas/terrorism

Southern Poverty Law Center
Tel: +1 334 956 8200
www.splcenter.org

The Terrorism Research Center
Tel: +1 877635 0816
Email: trc@terrorism.com
www.terrorism.com

Index